Spiritually Centered Motherhood

Spiritually Centered Motherhood

Sherrie Johnson

Bookcraft
Salt Lake City, Utah

Library of Congress Catalog Card Number: 83-70693
ISBN O-88494-478-6

2nd Printing, 1983

Lithographed in the United States of America
PUBLISHERS PRESS
Salt Lake City, Utah

To my parents
Ivo Dell Mills and Geraldine Young Mills
who sacrificed to give me life
and taught me how to live

"Therefore shall ye lay up these my words in your heart and in your soul....
And ye shall teach them your children, speaking of them when thou sittest in thine house, and when thou walkest by the way, when thou liest down, and when thou risest up." (Deuteronomy 11:18-19.)

Contents

Preface

I was the oldest of five children and was often given responsibility to tend my brothers and sisters. After many of these tending experiences, I'd complain to Mother about my siblings' behavior only to have her respond, "Just use a little psychology on them."

When I had children of my own, Mom's words came back to me and I turned to the child-rearing psychology books. These helped, but I still felt a void. Psychology wasn't enough. In order to return my children to their Father in Heaven, I felt I needed something more. So, as I had been taught to do when faced with a problem, I turned to the scriptures. As I studied I began to find ways to activate my own spiritual potential and gifts and those of each of my children. The difference this made was unbelievable.

Activating the spiritual potential, however, is not a job we as mothers do alone; spiritual training is a responsibility both husband and wife share. Because the bulk of the teaching falls to the woman, I have chosen to address these pages to mothers. The principles, however, are the same for both mothers and fathers, and more effective teaching can take place if a husband and wife discuss, agree upon, and then teach gospel principles together.

Motherhood and fatherhood are the most exciting, most rewarding, most challenging professions on the earth. But, more than that, they are the only professions that are eternal. Clearly, incorporating the concepts of the gospel more fully into our parenting will not only help us raise our children here in mortality, but will help prepare us for eternal parenthood. It is my hope that this book will make a small contribution to that objective.

Chapter 1

Spirituality Centered
Motherhood

"Build upon my rock, which is my gospel."
—D&C 11:24

The excruciating pains that periodically seized my body had kept me awake the entire night. I rolled over to look at the clock for the hundredth time. It was six o'clock—finally. Carefully I crawled out of bed. The pains were still only about eight minutes apart, but they had been hard enough to chase away any expectation of sleep.

"I think we'd better call the doctor," I told my husband, Carl.

"Are you sure?" he asked. I'd told him that three times during the previous week only to have the contractions stop shortly afterward.

"They're a lot harder this time."

Carl looked at me. I looked back. Unable to articulate what we were feeling, still we somehow sensed that our love, our relationship, was being reaffirmed and given new potential through this experience of pain and joy.

An hour later we arrived at the doctor's office, a strange mixture of fear and excitement pulsing through me.

By then the contractions were five minutes apart. "Go on over to the hospital and we'll have you a baby before noon," the doctor instructed.

Sensing that my life would never be the same again, I smiled through a pain. All of the days before this moment had been preparing me for all of the days that were to follow. Slowly the hours passed. Noon came and went, and anticipation and joy fought against the pain and fear. By then I wasn't sure this was worth it. Why had I wanted this so much? Why did there need to be such suffering? How could I stand another minute of this?

"Soon, soon!" the nurse kept reassuring. "Just be thankful you're not crossing the prairies in a covered wagon."

"I am. I am," I whispered through clenched teeth as the monstrous pain assaulted me again.

One o'clock slipped slowly by. I was just at the point of complete despair, having decided that the joys of motherhood were much overrated, when everything began to happen at once. At 2:05 P.M. the doctor held up a slimy, red, screaming baby. "It's a girl," he said, as if he'd done it all himself. "Healthy, vocal little girl."

Big tears welled up in my eyes. Joy pulsed through me in electric jolts. I had never seen or experienced anything so beautiful in all my life. "A mother is born," I kept thinking, "and it's me!"

Later, after I was comfortably situated in a room, they brought my daughter to me, washed and smelling like sweet springtime. As I took the warm bundle into my arms, a love unlike anything I had ever experienced surged through me. It didn't seem I could hold her tight enough. How could I possibly express what I was feeling? This was my daughter! I wanted to shout it from the housetops and at the same time savor and protect the secret.

"How will you ever know what I feel at this moment?" I whispered. "How can I let you know how much I love you?"

And then the feeling overcame me, "Teach her of Me."

That night, for the second night in a row, I lay exhausted but wide awake. Nurses with flashlights tiptoed periodically into the room. "You've got to sleep, Mrs. Johnson. Do you want another sleeping pill?"

"No," I answered. "It wouldn't do any good."

How could anyone sleep after what I had experienced? Happiness danced within me. Even with a sleeping pill, even after all those sleepless hours, I could not sleep. All I could do the entire night was repeat over and over a simple prayer, "Father, I thank thee."

Thus I began my sojourn as a mother. This precious first-born grew and Heavenly Father sent seven more daughters to our home. With each my joy increased, but there also came an increase in my overwhelming sense of responsibility to return these choice spirits, unblemished, to our Heavenly Father.

"Teach them of Me," the words kept coming back. I knew that was what I wanted to do—had to do. As the months passed my thoughts kept turning to the story in the Book of Mormon of the Ammonite mothers. These beautiful women raised two thousand young sons who joined Helaman to fight against the invading Lamanite armies.

Helaman said of them: "Now they never had fought, yet they did not fear death; and they did think more upon the liberty of their fathers than they did upon their lives; yea, they had been taught by their mothers, that if they did not doubt, God would deliver them. And they rehearsed unto me the words of their mothers, saying: We do not doubt our mothers knew it." (Alma 56:47-48.)

"Yea, and they did obey and observe to perform every word of command with exactness; yea, and even according to their faith it was done unto them; and I did remember the words which they said unto me that their mothers had taught them" (Alma 57:21).

Helaman went on to give these valiant young men credit for the Nephite victory, saying, "Now this was the faith of these of whom I have spoken; they are young, and their minds are firm, and they do put their trust in God continually" (Alma 57:27).

Every time I read or heard this account I marveled at the greatness of these mothers. But this was not the only story I found that inspired me. In the Old Testament I read of Rebekah, who realized that the most important thing in life was that she raise righteous children. Her son Esau had strayed and married outside the covenant. His twin, Jacob, was still unmarried and Rebekah worried that he too would stray.

"And Rebekah said to Isaac, I am weary of my life because of the daughters of Heth: if Jacob take a wife of the daughters of Heth, such as these which are of the daughters of the land, *what good shall my life do me?*" (Genesis 27:46; emphasis added.)

Besides these stories, I found in the scriptures many instructions for parents, such as: "Train up a child in the way he should go: and when he is old, he will not depart from it" (Proverbs 22:6); "But I have commanded you to bring up your children in light and truth" (D&C 93:40; see also 68:25-28 and Mosiah 4:14-15). And I also found warnings: "And that wicked one cometh and taketh away light and truth, through disobedience, from the children of men, and because of the tradition of their fathers" (D&C 93:39). The feeling of responsibility to teach my children correctly became even more intense as I pondered this scripture. Though I could not prevent them from disobeying the commandments if they ultimately chose to do so, I did have control over the traditions and teachings passed on to them. I did not want my children to stray because I had failed to teach them correctly.

As I pondered on these things, I realized that to raise children of God I could not rely upon the precepts of men. To raise a child of God I would need to use the words and ways of God.

I began to realize that it wasn't the Church's responsibility to teach my daughters. It was mine. So I turned to the scriptures and began gathering helps and insights as to how I should go about the task. One of the most significant insights came from Doctrine and Covenants 29:34, "Wherefore, verily I say unto you that all things unto me are spiritual."

As I pondered these words, I began to wonder how many of my problems were caused because I was trying to separate the temporal and the spiritual. If all things were spiritual unto the Lord then wouldn't my life be better if I tried to make all things spiritual to me?

To realize the change this made in my life, one must know how much I have always hated housework. I can tolerate vacuuming and ironing and sometimes come close to enjoying cooking, but I absolutely detest scrubbing walls and floors and cleaning ovens, stoves, and toilets. Yet, I recognize the importance of these things being done. Before, as I had worked, I'd find myself caught up in the detestableness of what I was doing, which brought on spells of self-pity and orneriness. But as I began to practice making everything spiritual, I gained great strength and power over my emotions. As I rinsed out dirty diapers in the toilet, instead of thinking about how I hated the task, I began to think about the beautiful baby I was lucky enough to be serving, about her angelic little smile, about her closeness to God and how much he loved her.

As I did this I began to discover that the difference between the temporal and spiritual is often just a difference in attitude. I was amazed and still marvel at the joy that comes from attempting to make all experiences spiritual, merely by trying to make all thoughts and actions Christlike. I can't say that I now love washing out diapers, or that housework has become a joy. No such miracle has taken place. But now I can be happy instead of miserable while doing these things, and I have found an inner peace I never had before.

As I began to make all things spiritual and to search the scriptures for help I coined a title to identify what I was striving to become: a *spiritually centered mother.* To me this is a mother who makes the gospel of Jesus Christ the center of her existence, who attempts to make all things spiritual to herself and her family. A spiritually centered mother not only teaches her children the gospel, she makes gospel principles part of their lives.

At first thought this may not be appealing to a lot of women. Too often society has tagged spirituality with dull, overpious, unsmiling, no-enjoyment associations. But if we look at the lives of righteous people, analyze the beautiful, exciting world the Lord has created for us, we soon realize these tags are part of Satan's work. Everything—*everything*—in life becomes more enjoyable, more exciting, more meaningful when we concentrate on the spiritual and gain the companionship of the Holy Ghost.

Once we overcome the old misrepresentations of what a spiritual person is, the thought of becoming a spiritually centered mother becomes an exciting challenge. I knew it was what I wanted, but the question that plagued me was, "How do I teach these things to my children?"

My scripture reading was giving me just enough answers to make me want more. The books I'd read on helping build my children's self-esteem or their intellectual capabilities gave me a basic guide or plan of things I must do to achieve those goals. But what steps did I need to take to develop spirituality in my children? What was the first thing I should teach them, and the second and third? How should I go about teaching them?

I still felt that the answers must be in the scriptures, but there was so much there I didn't know where to begin. I wanted a lesson plan or guide. Then one day, after some months of study and prayer, I was talking with a man about King Benjamin's great sermon in the Book of Mormon (Mosiah 2-5). As he told me about the steps he had found in the speech for personal conversion, firecrackers went off in my mind. "That's it!" I thought. "If King Benjamin could lift his people to the level of commitment he did in that one speech, how could my effectiveness be improved by using those same steps on a daily basis with my children?"

I went home and prayerfully began to study the speech. I paraphrased each verse in my own words. I read it over and over again. Then, after many weeks of prayer and study, I suddenly realized that everything in the speech fell into one of eight subjects:

1. Preparing to teach
2. Coming to know our Heavenly Father
3. Using agency
4. Learning about the Savior's mission
5. Inviting the Spirit into our lives
6. Living the law of consecration
7. Enduring to the end
8. Doing things in order

I labeled these the eight steps of teaching the gospel and continued searching the scriptures with these steps in mind. Before long I had a basic outline for teaching my children.

The material in this outline is not new. It is nothing more than the doctrine the prophets have taught through the ages. It is also not the only guide for teaching the gospel of Jesus Christ. It is merely a lesson plan that would allow me to evaluate my children's knowledge and give me direction as to what to teach next. My excitement came from having a concrete, orderly guide I could refer to that would help me teach the concepts of the gospel to my children a step at a time. Instead of trying to teach everything all at once I could concentrate on one step for a period of time and then go on to the next step. (How to apply and use the steps is described in more detail in chapter 9.)

The basic plan as found in the eight steps is what this book is all about. It is by no means comprehensive. Each person must study the scriptures and seek the Lord in prayer for a thorough understanding of gospel concepts and principles. This book is only a guide to help teach the gospel to children on a daily basis.

Chapter 2

Step One: Preparing to Teach

"Seek not to declare my word, but first seek to obtain my word, and then shall your tongue be loosed; then, if you desire, you shall have my Spirit and my word, yea, the power of God unto the convincing of men."—D&C 11:21

In the Book of Mormon we are told the story of Ammon, who went to the land of Ishmael to teach the gospel to the hostile Lamanites. As he entered the land, however, he was captured and carried to the king, Lamoni. When Lamoni learned that Ammon desired to dwell among the Lamanite people he was so pleased that he offered Ammon a wife from among his own daughters. "But Ammon said unto him: Nay, but I will be thy servant" (Alma 17:25).

Lamoni accepted this offer, sending Ammon into the fields with some of the other servants to tend the flocks. While they tended, a band of wicked Lamanites scattered the flocks. The servants began to murmur and weep; however, "when Ammon saw this his heart was swollen within him with joy; for, said he, I will show forth my power unto these my fellow-servants, or the power which is in me, in restoring these flocks unto the king, that I may win the hearts of these my fellow-servants, that I may lead them to believe in my words" (Alma 17:29).

Quickly gathering the flocks, Ammon instructed the servants to encircle them. He then approached the band of offending Lamanites and singlehandedly fought the robbers, cutting off the arms of those who raised their clubs against him. Finally Ammon drove the marauders away, then returned to water the flocks. The servants gathered the amputated arms, took them to the king, and told him everything that had happened. Lamoni was so astonished he exclaimed, "Surely, this is more than a man. Behold, is not this the Great Spirit?" (Alma 18:2.)

Lamoni then asked the servants where Ammon was. When they answered that he was preparing the horses and chariots as he had been commanded to do, King Lamoni was even more astonished because of Ammon's faithfulness.

By the time Ammon came into Lamoni's chamber, Lamoni was so overcome he could not speak. Ammon, by the power of the Spirit, perceived the situation and began teaching Lamoni the gospel. At this point Ammon had so completely won Lamoni's respect and love that Lamoni accepted the gospel as fast as Ammon could teach it.

This powerful story illustrates the importance of preparing relationships before we try to teach. Because we are mothers we are automatically teachers, but giving birth to a child does not naturally establish an *effective* teacher-learner relationship. As Ammon did, we must carefully cultivate and prepare the relationship before positive learning experiences can consistently happen.

As we study the examples of great teachers in the scriptures, we see that they developed the teacher-learner relationship in three distinct ways. These great teachers, including Jesus, became such because of their love for the people they were teaching, their gospel knowledge, and their self-discipline. These traits made them teachers by example as well as by word.

Loving Those We Teach

At first it may seem superfluous to discuss having love for the people we are teaching when those people are our own children. Of course we love them! We need to realize, however, that even when we love our children very much they may for various reasons fail to feel loved. The foundation for an effective teacher-learner situation is built not upon the amount of love we have, but on the amount our children feel.

Many guides and helps as to how to communicate love have been given to us by behavioral scientists. These guides include such things as learning to listen and empathizing with the child. These skills are very valuable and we would profit by learning and using them. But besides communication skills, honesty and forthrightness are important elements in our relationships with our children. If we truly love them we will accept them with all their shortcomings and will be willing to acknowledge our own faults as well.

A few years ago a teenage girl came to me very upset about her relationship with her mother. As she spilled both tears and words I began to see what the problem was. The mother was afraid to admit that she had any faults or shortcomings, or even that she had had any while growing. Perhaps she thought the girl would not respect or love her as much if she admitted to failings. Whatever the reason, it was causing the young girl a great deal of frustration. She saw faults in her mother, but the mother persisted in trying to hide and deny the faults. The daughter was beginning to rebel against what she felt was hypocrisy. Furthermore, she found it very difficult to confide her problems to a person who claimed never to have done anything wrong. She felt her mother couldn't identify with the problems or would condemn her for them. But the problem went even deeper. The girl felt that if faults were such a terrible thing to her mother, then her own faults and shortcomings must make her unwanted by and unacceptable to her mother.

Acknowledging our problems and demonstrating that we are trying to improve can only strengthen our relationships with our children. Repeatedly my children ask me to tell them about the time I disregarded the promptings of the Holy Ghost and lost my wallet with my entire savings in it. I've watched their faces as I tell the story and I know that they have learned from this and similar accounts. It is a great part of love to be able to say, "I'm sorry," or "I made a mistake," or "I'm only human, but I'm trying the best I can."

To give additional reinforcement to love, many families have found it fun as well as valuable to work out signals that express love. For instance, in our family three squeezes of the hands mean, "I love you." Four squeezes back mean, "I love you, too." We also use the deaf sign language to express love when words can't be used. The deaf sign for "I love you" is made by holding up the little finger and the index finger and extending the thumb, while folding down the middle and ring fingers. In a meeting, while waving goodbye to the children, or on numerous other occasions the signal has proved very useful.

One mother told me that she often calls to her son while he is at play, not to come and eat, not to finish his chores, not for any of the normal reasons. As he responds to her call she simply replies, "Son, I love you." She says it never fails to make the day go better for both of them.

We also express our love by being interested in the things that interest our children. One mother of a teenage son, a very cultured, sophisticated woman, told me that she felt her son growing away from her. To help solve the problem, she joined him under the hood of his car and had him teach her all about auto mechanics. Now not only does she know about carburetors, but her son has rediscovered his mom and has gained a new respect and renewed love for her. If we care enough to be interested, love finds a way to communicate.

I have often wondered what the world would be like if every time a child looked into his mother's face he saw love reflected there. That is possibly one of the best ways to make home a heaven on earth.

Love is a vast subject, and everyone's style of loving is different. Some mothers seem stern and cold to others, yet they effectively communicate love to their children. Some mothers are very affectionate and to the stern mother might even appear overindulgent. Some mothers run very formal homes, others have very relaxed, easygoing homes, but both kinds of mothers are able to communicate love; both kinds succeed.

The important thing is that our style of showing and expressing love is natural. If a mother tries to be something she is uncomfortable being, the child will sense it. This doesn't mean that we don't try to improve ourselves. Affection is necessary for children, and a mother who is too cold or stern must learn to be more affectionate. But she will still be working within the basic framework of her own personality in order to provide a real and consistent atmosphere of love for her children.

As we proceed through the eight steps of teaching our children the gospel, we find that the principles themselves build and encourage loving relationships. Because of this we will be discussing more aspects of love in other chapters.

Knowing the Gospel

The next area involved in becoming an effective teacher is gospel knowledge. President Marion G. Romney said, "God has a plan for building family stability, and that plan is revealed in the scriptures.... The Lord will help all of us to implement that plan." (*Ensign,* February 1972, page 62.)

In the book of Acts we are told that the people of Berea "were more noble than those in Thessalonica, in that they received the word with all readiness of mind, and *searched the scriptures daily"* (Acts 17:11; emphasis added). We are also told, "All scripture is given by inspiration of God, and is profitable for doctrine, for reproof, for correction, for instruction in righteousness: That the man of God may be perfect, throughly furnished unto all good works" (2 Timothy 3:16-17).

Gospel study includes study of the Bible, the Book of Mormon, the Doctrine and Covenants, the Pearl of Great Price, the words of modern prophets as printed in conference addresses, and our own patriarchal blessings. Some women pick a topic and research it. Others read straight through the standard works looking up footnotes and studying topics as they go. However we choose to work, the following steps taken from the scriptures themselves are helpful in making our study time more valuable.

1. "Feast upon the words of Christ; for behold, the words of Christ will tell you all things what ye should do" (2 Nephi 32:3). This first step is simply to read the scriptures, take them into our minds and hearts, devour the words, feast upon them.

2. "Wherefore, now after I have spoken these words, if ye cannot understand them it will be because ye ask not, neither do ye knock; wherefore, ye are not brought into the light, but must perish in the dark" (2 Nephi 32:4). We need to pray to understand the things we are reading, but it does not end there. We must also pray to be able to incorporate the things we learn into our lives. Studying the scriptures without praying is like brushing our teeth without toothpaste. If we ask in prayer, we will be better able to understand the things we read.

3. "And I did read many things unto them which were written in the books of Moses; but that I might more fully persuade them to believe in the Lord their Redeemer I did read unto them that which was written by the prophet Isaiah; for I did liken all scriptures unto us, that it might be for our profit and learning" (1 Nephi 19:23). As we read we might ask ourselves such questions as, "How does this apply

to my life?" "How can this story help me?" "What can I learn from this verse?" "How does this apply to modern days?" Likening the scriptures to our own situation is the key to making the gospel come alive for us. Asking pertinent questions opens new doors to scriptural symbolism, meaning, and application.

4. "Therefore, go ye unto your homes, and ponder upon the things which I have said, and ask of the Father, in my name, that ye may understand, and prepare your minds for the morrow, and I come unto you again" (3 Nephi 17:3). Pondering or meditating becomes a special part of learning the gospel. As we read, we need to stop from time to time and savor the thoughts in our minds. This gives the Spirit an opportunity to teach us and to expound on the things we are reading. At the end of our day's study, we can also ponder for a few minutes on what we have learned, to give the thoughts time to sink from the mind into the heart.

Many times in studying or teaching the gospel we concentrate on the stories and facts: "Who were Mosiah's sons?" "How many days was Noah in the ark?" These things often add interest, but they are merely historical facts, not gospel insights. It is not until we move to the levels of pondering and likening that we really learn the gospel.

Another reason we ponder the scriptures is to discover their rich symbolism. Quickly reading a story or passage does not allow the symbolism to come alive in our minds. If we ponder the meaning, the Spirit will lead us to discover new insights and knowledge contained in the symbolism. We are told in 2 Nephi 11:4 that all things given by God typify Christ. In meditating we also learn if we ask ourselves, "What does this teach me about Christ?"

Other questions, such as, "Why is this verse or story included?" or "What is the Lord trying to teach?" also help the pondering process. Another helpful exercise is comparing the verse to what precedes and follows and asking, "Why is this included in this particular place?" Other times using a dictionary to get exact definitions of words opens up whole new worlds of meaning.

5. "For my soul delighteth in the scriptures, and my heart pondereth them, and writeth them for the learning and the profit of my children" (2 Nephi 4:15). If daily scripture study has not been a part of our lives, then at first the reading may be tedious and difficult to understand. But if we persist until we can truly say we love the scriptures, then we too will be able to delight in these words of the Lord. True delight comes from experiencing the change in our lives that results from persistent, consistent scripture study.

In studying our patriarchal blessings we can do these same things. These blessings are conditional; their fulfillment depends upon our righteousness. They are scripture only to the individual they are given to and are important for guidance and direction. Besides reading, praying, and meditating about our blessings often, we benefit by occasionally "dissecting" our blessings in order to gain additional insights.

To do this I divide a piece of paper into five columns: 1. Information, 2. Counsel, 3. Gifts, 4. Warnings, and 5. Promises. I read through my blessing and list each thing in it under the appropriate heading. By doing this about once a year, I gain many new insights and added guidance and direction.

As to the physical task of daily study, some women enjoy studying in the quiet of the morning before the other household members are awake. One woman even said she likes to get up at three o'clock in the morning, study for an hour, and then go back to bed until six! Other women enjoy studying just before bedtime. It doesn't really matter when we study just as long as we do study. Sometimes it takes a period of experimenting to find which time of day or night allows us to effectively take the five steps, but if we persist we can make scripture study a habit. And any person who has made it a daily habit will testify to the strength and power it brings to a person's life. Questions answered, motivation to do better, and guidance and direction are just some of the blessings reaped from daily scripture study.

Perhaps the greatest blessing, however, is contained in the simple law that the more we know the more we can teach. Once the price of study has been paid and the knowledge gathered, the little but profound teaching moments often just naturally happen. At other times they can be brought about by slight manipulations.

As an example, almost every child at some time or other announces emphatically that he doesn't want to say his prayers. When this happens, one mother I know tells her children about Daniel. She explains how his peers were jealous of him and wanted to get him into trouble, so they proposed that King Darius enact a law that for thirty days no one could pray or worship anyone or anything except the king. Anyone who broke this law would be cast into a den of hungry lions. King Darius liked the idea and signed the law. The mother then reads to her children, "Now when Daniel knew that the writing was signed, he went into his house; and his windows being open in his chamber toward Jerusalem, he kneeled upon his knees three times a day, and prayed, and gave thanks before his God, as he did aforetime" (Daniel 6:10).

She then asks her children, "If prayer was so important to Daniel that he prayed three times a day even though he knew the penalty was death, then don't you think prayer should be just as important to us?" After talking about why prayer is so important, the child is usually ready to pray.

There are many other ways we can use the scriptures. During sacrament meeting several years ago our ward choir began singing, "O That I Were an Angel." Quickly I turned to Alma 29:1 and gave my Book of Mormon to Laresa so she could follow the words. She was very impressed and after the meeting asked many questions about why Alma wanted to be an angel. She would never have been so inquisitive if she had only heard the song. Since then I have made a list in the back of my scriptures of verses that have been set to music so that I can find them for the children when we hear them sung.

Self-Discipline

The third area in developing the teacher-learner relationship is that of self-discipline. Self-discipline can be defined as making the body obey the spirit. It is through self-discipline that we draw closer to our Father in Heaven and become like him. Just as physical exercise makes the body stronger, self-discipline makes the spirit stronger.

My husband and I had an interesting experience that helped us realize the importance of self-discipline. We had come to a point in our marriage where somehow because of our busy schedules we were growing apart instead of closer. We weren't communicating, and were becoming a little short-tempered with each other. It was not yet a serious problem, but I worried that it could become serious. I didn't like the direction we were headed in, and wanted to turn things around. I wanted more of the joy and happiness I knew a marriage should give.

Carl and I discussed the problem and tried to set a few goals that would help, but instead the problem got worse. Finally I decided to fast and pray about it. As I approached the end of my fast period, and after several prayers, I knelt down and prayed again to know what to do, listened, but got no answer. I went about my work and a little while later prayed again. This time I received no answer as to what to do, but was given the distinct feeling that my fast should end.

Past experience had taught me that the Lord doesn't always answer my prayers in the way I want or expect, so I ended my fast. That night, as we were getting ready for bed,

Carl, unaware that I had been fasting, told me that something extraordinary had happened to him that day. During the day he had been suddenly and forcibly struck with the thought that we should start exercising together.

I told him about my fasting and we realized that his answer had come at the same time I had been praying. We were baffled. How could exercise be the answer to our marriage problems? Nevertheless we discussed how to implement the command and the next morning at five-thirty we began jogging together. There seemed to be no logic to the answer we had received, but we continued to do as we had been personally commanded. It wasn't long before our relationship reached a point of strength and fulfillment that we had never before enjoyed.

As time passed and we discussed the phenomenon, we realized that what we had been lacking was self-discipline. We no longer exercise together, but we each exercise alone and the discipline we gain from making ourselves do something that is hard for us to do carries over into the other areas of our lives.

President David O. McKay said, "Spirituality is the consciousness of victory over self, and of communion with the Infinite." (*Gospel Ideals* [Salt Lake City: Improvement Era, 1953], page 390.) It is very significant that victory over self comes first. We need to recognize self-discipline as a basic part of spirituality. In order to grow close to our Father in Heaven, we must overcome the things of this world. We must have spirits that are stronger than our bodies, stronger than mortal appetites and passions.

It is possible to teach from whatever level of life we are on, but to truly lift someone we must be able to set an example of what we teach. The higher we climb, the more disciplined we are, the more potential we have to lift and inspire our children and those around us.

Brigham Young once said, "If a mother wishes to control her child, in the first place let her learn to control herself."

(*Journal of Discourses*, 14:277.) This is the meat of the issue. If we are to establish a relationship of love and learning, we must first learn to control ourselves. This control allows us to set examples our children can follow.

Another important aspect of self-discipline is that it builds self-esteem and allows us to be at peace with ourselves, thereby freeing us from inner turmoil and allowing us to concentrate on our children's needs. A woman who is not at peace with herself, who has never learned who she is or where she is going, who has not mastered herself, and who does not like herself cannot effectively teach her children because of her own distress.

What is perhaps the most important reason for self-discipline is the one we touched on a few paragraphs back. If we are not disciplined we cannot be responsive to the promptings of the Holy Ghost. The more we discipline ourselves—the more control we have over ourselves—the closer we are to the Spirit. When we control our appetites, passions, and tempers, we open the door to communication with the Spirit because we have gained the ability to act upon the promptings the Spirit gives us.

Children are a mother's chief stewardship. Our desire is to do everything in our power to teach them. "And whoso is found a faithful, a just, and a wise steward shall enter into the joy of his Lord, and shall inherit eternal life" (D&C 51:19).

Summing Up

We must establish an effective teacher-learner relationship:
1. by making our love known.
2. by gaining gospel knowledge through daily scripture study by—
   a. feasting upon the words of the scriptures,
   b. praying for understanding of the scriptures,
   c. likening the scriptures to our own situations,

    d. pondering and meditating on what we read,

    e. delighting in the scriptures, realizing that they are for our profit and learning.

3. by disciplining ourselves so that we become examples of what we teach.

Chapter 3

Step Two: Coming to Know Our Heavenly Father

"And it came to pass that Moses looked upon Satan and said: Who art thou? For behold, I am a son of God, in the similitude of his Only Begotten; and where is thy glory, that I should worship thee?"—Moses 1:13

A friend of mine was left alone with three young children, the baby just six weeks old, while her husband served in the armed forces in Korea. While he was gone the husband often sent home pictures of himself that the children could play with, and the mother repeatedly told them stories about their father and did everything she could to keep a memory of him alive in the children.

When the father returned after thirteen months in Korea, the youngest child was the first to see him come through the door. The baby's face beamed and his eyes twinkled as he ran to his father, threw his chubby arms out for a hug, and exclaimed excitedly, "Daddy, Daddy!"

The child had been only six weeks old when his father had left, yet his recognition and excitement upon the reunion reflected great love and familiarity with his father. There is much we can learn from this woman. Think of the strength

22

we could give our families by bringing our Heavenly Father as close to each child as this woman brought her absent husband to her children.

Joseph Smith taught, "Our only confidence can be in God; our only wisdom obtained from Him; and He alone must be our protector and safeguard, spiritually and temporally, or we fall." (*Teachings of the Prophet Joseph Smith* [Salt Lake City: Deseret Book, 1976], page 253.)

In order for our children to have this kind of trust and confidence in God, several things must happen. First, a child must gain a testimony that God is literally the father of his spirit.

A Divine Heritage

In the Pearl of Great Price there is an account of God appearing to Moses. "And God spake unto Moses, saying: Behold, I am the Lord God Almighty, and Endless is my name; for I am without beginning of days or end of years; and is not this endless? And, behold, thou art my son." (Moses 1:3-4.)

During this experience God went on to reveal many great and important things to Moses, and throughout the recorded part of the revelation he continued to address Moses, almost without exception, as "my son." Then, after the presence of the Lord withdrew, Moses fell helplessly to the ground. For many hours he lay, his strength completely gone. While he was in this weakened condition, "Satan came tempting him, saying: Moses, son of man, worship me" (Moses 1:12).

It is extremely significant that the first thing Satan did was attempt to undermine Moses' testimony of his divine heritage. If Satan could convince Moses that he was only of earthly origin, not of divine origin, he could then persuade Moses to do his evil bidding. But Moses was not deceived. "And it came to pass that Moses looked upon Satan and said:

Who art thou? For behold, *I am a son of God,* in the similitude of his Only Begotten; and where is thy glory, that I should worship thee?" (Moses 1:13; emphasis added.)

What strength our children would have if their testimonies of their divine origin were as well founded as this. If a child really feels and knows that he is a child of God and that God loves and cares for him, his response to temptation may also be: "Behold, I am a child of God! I will not do such a thing!"

Every Latter-day Saint can tell you he is a child of God. At home, in Primary, and elsewhere the thought has been programmed into his mind. As mothers our job is to move the thought from the mind to the heart. It must be more than a saying to the child; it must be part of his testimony. It must be part of his definition of himself. It must be a real emotional and spiritual conviction.

The day after a home evening lesson in which we had discussed being children of God, our daughter Breana, then five years old, lingered at the table while I cleared away the lunch dishes. She sat quietly, her big blue eyes intense, her forehead wrinkled in thought. Finally she spoke, "Mom, is it really true that I am a child of God?"

"Yes," I assured her. She sat silently for many more minutes, a perplexed look filling her face.

"And is it true that you are a child of God?"

"Yes," I answered.

Suddenly the questioning expression changed to a grin as she excitedly announced, "Then that means we are sisters!"

The learning moment was then mine as waves of thought flooded my mind and emotions. Intellectually I'd always known that we were spirit sisters, but at that moment I *felt* that we were sisters. This new perspective was an added testimony to me that I am a daughter of God.

This concept increases in importance when we realize that as we teach a child of his heavenly heritage we also teach him of his heavenly potential. When a person has a testimony that he is a child of a Heavenly Father, he can also gain a testimony that he can become like his Heavenly Father. That testimony in and of itself is a great blessing. Life with its burdens and cares becomes much more tolerable when the hope of greater and better things—of godhood—is a firm conviction.

We begin teaching this concept to a child the day he is born. A child who knows he is loved and valued as an individual can easily believe he is a child of God. But a child with low self-esteem, one who feels unloved and unwanted, cannot believe that he has such a divine heritage.

From the first day of life a child begins to form an opinion of how much his parents love him, of how much he is wanted or valued. If he is cuddled tenderly and carefully he feels differently than if he is jostled like a bag of vegetables. As he grows the treatment he receives continues to say either, "You are important to me," or "You are not worth my time and attention." Little things, things that seem insignificant at the time, are usually the most important communicators of these feelings of worth. A mother who puts down what she is doing when her child comes home, and really listens to his account of the day, is saying, "You matter to me." Empathizing with a child's problems, no matter how insignificant they may seem, says, "I care."

There are many more areas we could discuss whereby we build our children's self-esteem, but again the scriptures have given us the best key to making our children feel worthwhile and loved. In all our dealings with them we need only apply the Golden Rule and treat them as we would like to be treated. That doesn't mean that we give them everything they want, but that with the wisdom of maturity we give them what is best for them. That is what we would want someone else to do for us. If we do this for our children, they will feel loved and valued. They will feel worthwhile. They will *feel* like children of God.

But, as with all of the concepts we teach, if we do not first take this step for ourselves it is hard to teach it. Many parents have trouble building their children's self-esteem because they themselves are so insecure. Their interactions with a child are calculated to feed their own egos instead of the child's. They are disappointed when the child fails in public because they feel it makes them look bad. This is a dangerous position for a mother to be in. Children soon catch on to the fact that they can manipulate a parent through the parent's insecurities. They learn that they can cry in a public place and have mother give in to their demands in order to avoid embarrassment. They learn that if they tell mother how neat a friend's parent is, mother will try to outdo the popular parent. The list goes on and on.

For us to avoid these snares, our self-esteem must be secure enough that we are not dependent upon our children to feed our egos. We must not be hurt when our children deflate us.

If we do not like ourselves, we can do several things to improve our self-concepts. The most important is to pray for help and guidance. Scripture study and fasting also help. These things bring us closer to our Father in Heaven and help develop in us the testimony that we are children of God and that he loves us.

Stressing the Spiritual

In teaching the children of their divine heritage, we in our home life should also stress and concentrate on the spiritual part of each person. If as parents we stress and value such traits as integrity, honesty, love, kindness, modesty, and sincerity, we will build and encourage the internal or spiritual side of each child—the part that is a child of God. But if we only value and encourage traits such as physical beauty, fashion consciousness, popularity, athletic ability, or material status, we build and encourage external qualities that are a temporal part of each child—qualities that belong to man.

When we seek external qualities with no root or motivation from the spiritual part of our lives, we find ourselves doing right things for wrong reasons and moving in wrong directions. But when the spiritual or internal qualities are stressed and developed, the temporal ambitions are controlled by the spiritual and we do right things for right reasons. As we feel our internal or spirit selves growing and developing, it is easier for us to feel like children of God.

Characteristics of Heavenly Father

Besides teaching a child of his divine heritage, we should also teach him the correct attributes and characteristics of his Heavenly Father. A child cannot love and trust in a Heavenly Father he does not know. The Prophet Joseph Smith instructed: "Having a knowledge of God, we begin to know how to approach him, and how to ask so as to receive an answer. When we understand the character of God, and know how to come to him, he begins to unfold the heavens to us, and to tell us all about it. When we are ready to come to him, he is ready to come to us." (*Teachings of the Prophet Joseph Smith*, page 350.)

We can begin to teach our children about their Heavenly Father by teaching them that God has a body of flesh and bone and that they are created in his image. They must understand that he is perfect and all-knowing, and that he understands what they are going through. But most of all they must know that he wants them to succeed in their earthly mission so they can return to him. He knows their purpose in life. He knows all about them; therefore he can guide and direct them better than anyone else could.

Omniscience

Some children and even adults have trouble understanding how God can know all things, how he can know the end from the beginning, how he can know what we will do and still permit us to exercise agency. Our children must understand that God's foreknowledge does not mean that he makes things happen the way they do. They are the ones that choose what will happen to them. If they understand this concept they can then trust in God to direct them throughout their lives, and will also understand what he means when he says he will not allow us to be tried beyond our capacity. He knows our purpose in life, he knows our strengths and gifts and will help us discover these things. He knows our weaknesses and will help us overcome them, but at all times we must be the ones to choose and to act upon our choices. He can only guide and direct us.

To help my children understand this concept, I have used an example that is easily adaptable to any family's experience. I have my daughters imagine that while Laresa is out of the room I will fix three breakfasts: oatmeal mush, french toast, and fried eggs. We pretend that she comes into the room to pick her breakfast. Before she even enters the room to see what is available, however, I know what she will choose: the french toast. I have a foreknowledge of her choice, but that knowledge in no way infringes upon her ability or freedom to choose. Now, if I in my limited human state can know my daughter this well, how much better can God know us?

Our Heavenly Father knows all about us, but that does not mean he sets our way or charts our course. We do that by our choices. We need to travel through mortality in order to gain the spiritual strength and faith necessary for us to become gods ourselves. Here we prove ourselves to ourselves and gain faith by our choices.

Love

Another important thing to teach our children is that Heavenly Father created them and he loves and cares for them. He is a personal Father. He knows all of us by name, but more than that he knows how we feel and he loves us very much.

To help my children understand Heavenly Father's love for them, I like to brainstorm with them the things that might have happened as he sent us here. I am careful to explain that we do not know exactly what took place in our premortal life, and that what we imagine is not necessarily what did happen, but that we do know how very much our Father loves us. Then we imagine together. I try to steer the conversation so that the emphasis is not on the circumstances, but on the feelings we must have had.

These sessions are very special, and we hold them only occasionally so that they do not lose that specialness. Still, at other times the feelings are brought back as one of us remembers our brainstorming or refers to some of the things we talked about.

Law

In coming to know the attributes of our Heavenly Father, our children must also learn that there are certain things even Heavenly Father cannot do. His perfection of attributes makes it impossible for him to break eternal laws, to break his covenants with us, or to do or produce anything evil. And since our eternal rewards are based upon spiritual laws, he cannot grant us celestial life if we do not obey the commandments, even though he loves us deeply. It is impossible. As he has told us, "I, the Lord, am bound when ye do what I say; but when ye do not what I say, ye have no promise" (D&C 82:10).

Heavenly Father is who he is partly because he has learned to live completely within the law. Even when, as with what we call a miracle, he seems to intervene to give us a special blessing, we can be sure he is operating by a higher law we do not understand in our present state of development.

Often we hear young people say, "If Heavenly Father really loves us, why does he let pain and suffering happen?"

Or, as a nonmember once told me, "If Heavenly Father loves us, why doesn't he just let us all into heaven? I can't believe he'll only let those baptized in your church into heaven."

Such a statement reflects lack of understanding. Particularly in the spiritual realm, God must allow the consequences of a broken law to happen. He cannot prevent or alter those consequences, otherwise, as Alma tells us, "God would cease to be God" (Alma 42:22). He can only teach us what the laws are and then help and encourage us to live them.

We need to teach our children this principle. When a child understands that Heavenly Father cannot commute the laws, it is easier for him to understand that Heavenly Father has given us commandments because he loves us. A good illustration of that point is this object lesson: Ask the children to imagine you have a great, fantastic gift for them, but in order to receive the gift they must go to Venice. Explain that in the world there must be at least thirty cities named Venice. Give them a moment to think about it and then ask if they would be upset if you told them which Venice was the correct one and gave them a map that would show them exactly how to get there. When they say no, you can explain that the commandments are like a "map" to guide us to the celestial kingdom. If we follow the commandments we will receive a greater gift than anything that is upon the earth. Explain that we should not feel restricted by the commandments, but that, like a treasure map, they are a tremendous help to us. Commandments are given to us because our Heavenly Father loves us so much that he wants us to live with him forever. They are a priceless gift that enables us to seek after the blessings of God. Without the commandments we would stumble and lose our way. We would never know what to do to inherit the celestial kingdom.

Another way to teach this is to compare the commandments to food. As we eat food we gain physical strength; as we keep the commandments we gain spiritual strength. No one gets upset because he cannot eat a rubber tire. He knows it would not taste good or be good for his body. So why do we feel restricted when told to keep the Sabbath holy? Breaking the Sabbath is just as harmful to the spirit as eating a rubber tire would be to the body. Without the commandments we would literally starve to death spiritually, just as we would starve physically without food.

Fatherhood

As we study and teach the attributes of our Heavenly Father, we should also notice how he deals with us, his children. Stop and think for a moment about the responsibilities inherent in godhood. A god multiplies and replenishes worlds with his spirit offspring. A god creates a home or world for his children, teaches, guides, loves, succors, and provides a way for his children to grow and mature. Everything God does he does because he is a Father. Are any of these things different than what we are attempting to do in a simplified version as earthly parents? Godhood is parenthood perfected. Therefore, the more we understand our Heavenly Father and his ways, the more we learn about how we should deal with our own children. In addition we should realize that earthly parenthood is training for godhood. As we comfort, guide, teach, and aid our children, we are learning and developing traits that are necessary for us to become gods ourselves.

Prayer

The next thing we should teach our children is that the way we communicate with our Heavenly Father is through prayer. Doctrine and Covenants 68:28 says, "And they shall also teach their children to pray, and to walk uprightly before the Lord."

Prayer is one of the things that will motivate a child to walk uprightly before the Lord. But for it to motivate, prayer must be a meaningful part of each child's day, not just a collection of words. It must flow from the heart, not just the mind. We should teach our children to say whatever is in their hearts and to pray not only morning and night, but whenever they feel the need. As we encourage our children to talk with their Heavenly Father, to pour out their hearts, desires, and thanks to him, they will come to know him. They will from experience learn that for prayer to be effective it must be accompanied by an arousal of one's faculties. Words alone are not a prayer.

President Harold B. Lee said: "The most important thing you can do is to learn to talk to God. Talk to Him as you would talk to your father, for He is your Father, and He wants you to talk to Him. He wants you to cultivate ears to listen, when He gives you the impressions of the Spirit." (*Church News*, March 3, 1973, page 3.)

When our small children become frightened in the night, my husband and I say a little prayer with them asking Father to comfort them and take away the fear. As the children have grown and come to us in the middle of the night complaining of thunder or a dream or noise or any of the many nighttime scares, we express our love and concern, give them a hug and a kiss, and instruct them to go back to bed, kneel down, and pray.

I know I could go with them, tuck them in, and comfort away the scare, but I do not want them to be dependent upon me. I want them to learn to depend on their Heavenly Father. My powers to protect and aid are limited; his are not.

As the children have grown older they have ceased to even arouse us. The next morning they'll matter-of-factly explain that during the night they got scared, but they prayed and went back to sleep.

Once one of our daughters was having trouble with some friends. To be honest, we didn't know exactly how to advise her for this particular situation. The problem was a complicated one involving several very diverse personalities. After giving it a great deal of thought and prayer, we advised her to be patient and to pray about the problem. She made it part of her daily prayers and fasted about it. Whenever the problem came up she said a quick silent prayer to ask for help in dealing with the situation. A problem that could have had long-term consequences of self-deprecation turned out to be a faith-promoting experience that brought her closer to her Heavenly Father.

There are many situations such as these in which we should lovingly direct our children to their Heavenly Father instead of trying to handle all their trials ourselves. As we do this, Heavenly Father becomes real to them and they come not only to depend upon him but to love and trust him. However, we must lead them to him lovingly, never with the feeling that we don't care or that we can't be bothered to help them ourselves. We must always stress that we do care, that we love them dearly, but that Heavenly Father can help them much better than we can. We have human limitations and failings, but their Heavenly Father is all-powerful. He understands their needs and knows what is best for them.

Another aspect of praying that we should teach our children is to listen for a few moments after their prayer is said. Listening is the most important part of prayer. It doesn't make any sense to ask for answers and then close our prayer and jump into bed. To get an answer to prayer we must listen to the promptings and feelings within us. The quiet moments of listening allow the Spirit to speak to us.

One night while kissing five-year-old Anissa good night, I started to review the process of how to pray and then listen, only to have her raise her little hand and interrupt. "I know, I know, I always do that," she said, waving her hand to stop me from saying more, "because once when I listened Heavenly Father said, 'I love you'!"

As we teach about prayer, we must also teach that answers do not always come the first time we ask, or in the way we expect them. Sometimes many, many prayers and much time go by before we get an answer. I remember as a young girl praying and yearning for a best friend. Every night as I said my prayers I pleaded for the Lord to send me a friend that I could be close to and do things with, someone I could talk to. For almost two years I continued to pray for a special friend, but I didn't give up praying. Then one day a girl my age moved into a house just down the street. The day she moved in I met her and from that moment until now we have been special friends. I don't understand why it took so long for this prayer to be answered, but I do know that it was answered.

Family prayers are also very important. They should not be so long that young children learn to resent them, but they should not be a hurried, let's-get-this-over-with event either. Some families sing a song or hymn before prayer to get them into the proper mood. Our family has found that just a little quiet conversation before prayer helps set the tone. Usually my husband asks the family members if there is anything they would like mentioned in the prayer. The person called upon to offer the prayer includes these things so each family member feels part of the prayer.

We also need to stress to our children that prayer is a time for thanking our Father in Heaven. Too many times we think of prayer as an asking time, but it is also a thanking time. Jesus, when he visited the Nephites, said a prayer of thanks each time the things he had prayed for were granted. (Reading the account in 3 Nephi 19 with emphasis on verses 20 and 28 is helpful in teaching of giving thanks, and 3 Nephi 18:18-21 is helpful in teaching of prayer.)

Besides being one of the most important things we teach our children, prayer is the most important concept for us to follow in becoming spiritually centered mothers. No problem, if it is a problem to us, is too small or too large to be taken to the Lord.

One mother told of a time when her son was about ten years old. He had wanted and needed a close friend for some time, so when a group of neighborhood boys invited him to go trick or treating he was especially excited. On Halloween day, however, he came home from school utterly dejected. The friends had told him that the group was too large and that he couldn't go with them.

The mother's heart ached as she saw the pain reflected in her son's eyes. It wasn't the first time the group had mistreated him. She knew how anxiously he had looked forward to the event, and now he was shattered. He was too young to go alone and too old to go with mother, but more importantly, he needed a friend. The mother, as she was accustomed to doing, quietly slipped away to her bedroom, shut the door, and knelt down. She then proceeded to pour out her heart to her Father in Heaven. She told him that she knew how hurt and offended her son was and that he needed a special friend. "Show me what to do to help him," she prayed. Her prayer was interrupted by the ringing of the doorbell. She closed her prayer to answer the door and was greeted by a young neighborhood boy who wanted her son to go trick or treating with him. Not all prayers are answered so fast, but all prayers are answered. That is why prayer is one of the most valuable tools we can learn to use as mothers.

Our Father in Heaven loves us. We cannot stress that fact enough. He has told us that even a hair of our heads does not fall unnoticed. He has also said, "Ask and ye shall receive." The problem is that sometimes after he has told us, "No, the thing you are asking for is not for your best good," we give up. Instead of recognizing and accepting a no answer, we think that he is not there, that he doesn't hear our prayers. We must learn to listen, to recognize even the no answers, then continue in faith to ask for our needs to be met according to the Lord's will.

Studying the Scriptures

Scripture study is also an important part of coming to know our Heavenly Father. The scriptures are the word of

God, and more than any one thing will help our children come to know him and to love him. As we discussed in chapter 2, daily personal study is necessary as we develop our own testimonies. Likewise, family scripture study will help our children gain testimonies. Some families read in the morning; some read together at night. Some read one or two chapters a day; some read five or ten verses. Others even hold two sessions, one for the older children and one for the younger. The particular method of study does not much matter. Each family must experiment and find what suits their lifestyle and the ages of their children. But in teaching a child the gospel, and incorporating that gospel into his life, scripture study is extremely helpful.

Fasting

The proper way to fast is also an important thing to teach our children in order for them to draw closer to their Heavenly Father. Fasting means combining a prayerful attitude with abstinence from food and drink, usually for twenty-four hours. In an emergency, when the notice is brief, it could be a shorter fast. It could be shorter also for young children who are learning to fast. (Neither children nor anyone else should ever be "forced to fast" in any case. Example and gentle teaching are the keys here.) Feeling the spiritual need, some carry out longer fasts, after twenty-four hours continuing to abstain from food but taking needed liquids. More than one prophet, however, has indicated that it is not normally necessary to fast longer than twenty-four hours at a time when seeking a blessing.

Fasting gives us spiritual strength, builds faith, and is one of the best ways to grow close to our Father in Heaven. But when I am pregnant or nursing a baby I cannot fast. During these times I used to miss this great source of spiritual renewal. Then one day a friend who is a diabetic explained how she fasts. She refrains from any between-meal nibbling and also fasts from two or three of her favorite foods even at mealtime so that she still has the feeling of making her spirit obey and of exercising self-discipline by keeping her appetite under control. I tried doing the same thing and found that it works. Our Father in Heaven understands and, seeing our honest desire, accepts our efforts.

We should also teach our children that merely going without food is not fasting. When we fast we should have a specific purpose in mind. Each Fast Sunday my husband and I encourage our children—those who are old enough to fast—to choose something to fast and pray about. It can be something very specific, such as asking for a sick loved one to be made well, or for help with a personal problem. Other times the purpose may be more general: Asking for spiritual strength or that the Spirit will be with them is appropriate. They should not have to tell anyone what they are fasting for unless they want to.

A fast should begin and end in prayer. This not only adds strength and power to the fast, but it distinguishes it from a day when for some reason a meal is inadvertently missed. A child can be encouraged to find a spot where he can be alone for a few minutes to pray, keeping in mind his chosen purpose for the fast. We also have a family prayer together before breaking our fasts on Fast Sunday. During times of personal fasting, I pray not only to open and close the fast, but often many, many times in between. On Fast Sunday, however, I am usually so occupied with helping the family to fast, and trying to keep their thoughts on the right things, that there is little if any time for me to meditate and pray about the things I am fasting for, to really draw close to my Heavenly Father. Because of this I usually pick one day during the month to fast when there will be as few interruptions as possible. Then I am the only one fasting, the children are occupied with other things, and I can schedule my time during the fast period to include scripture study, meditation, and prayer. It is during these times that I feel closest to my

Heavenly Father, and also during these times I have come to know how much he loves and cares for me.

Summing Up

In teaching our children of their Heavenly Father, we must teach them:
1. that they are literally spirit children of God and that they have the potential to become like him.
2. the correct characteristics and attributes of our Heavenly Father.
3. how to commune with our Heavenly Father through prayer and fasting.

Chapter 4

Step Three: Using Our Agency

> *"Therefore, cheer up your hearts, and remember that ye are free to act for yourselves—to choose the way of everlasting death or the way of eternal life."—2 Nephi 10:23*

In the premortal life we fought a war to preserve a gift, a tremendous power, that we knew was very precious. This great gift—the gift of agency—allows us to choose how we deal with life's situations and enables us to gain the faith we need in order to return to our Father in Heaven. It allows us to choose our own eternal destination. But in order for that destination to be the celestial kingdom, we have to use agency properly. That is why learning to use agency is such a crucial part of spiritual development.

I once heard a man remark, "There is no such thing as a lazy person, only a person who does not understand the principle of agency." At first I wasn't sure I knew what he meant, but as I learned more about the principle of agency his meaning became very clear.

Agency involves the ability to choose between good and evil, or in other words, to make moral choices. Along with the right to make moral choices, however, exercising agency means that we must abide by the consequences of those choices. In other words, we may choose to obey or disobey a law, but in doing either we have chosen the consequences that will follow our choice and we cannot change them.

Agency vs. Freedom

To further consider agency, we need to realize that agency is not identical with freedom. Agency is a mental-spiritual power and its use always involves a moral choice—a choice between good and evil, right and wrong. Such a choice has spiritual consequences—potentially eternal ones, usually.

Freedom, on the other hand, though its exercise involves a mental decision, frequently has to do with lack of limitations on one's physical movement. Sometimes it involves following through on the use of agency—as in freedom of religion, which is permitted in different degrees in different countries. Frequently no moral choice is involved at all. It is the latter application I illustrate to simplify for my children the difference between agency and freedom.

In such an illustration we can use an example of an LDS girl in a store. This girl has a choice between buying and wearing a modest dress or an immodest dress. Because a commandment has been given, this is a moral decision. The girl can be obedient to the command to be modest or she can disobey and be immodest. She uses her agency to decide what she will do and then she acts from that decision and reaps the consequences.

In the case of freedom, the girl again has two choices, but there is no moral decision to make. In this case she will choose between a modest green dress and a modest blue dress. There is still a choice, but her agency is not involved; the choice is not between right and wrong but merely between two rights, or even two neutrals. She has her freedom to select either dress but there are no eternal consequences to the decision.

Any time we are deciding between a green or blue dress, Satan doesn't care; but when the choice is between modesty or immodesty, he takes an interest because he has something to gain by a wrong decision. If he can entice us to choose the immodest dress, he has, at least until we repent, hindered our progression. He has restricted our freedom to progress spiritually.

Another difference between agency and freedom is that our agency cannot be taken away from us. No matter how sinful a person becomes, he still has his agency in this life and at any time can choose to repent and change. However, a person's freedom can be taken away. Satan knows this, and he works at obtaining the next best thing to agency—our freedom. If he can entice us to make wrong choices these may result in wrong, addictive habits and behavior. Thus he begins to gain control of our freedom, and we are measurably in bondage to him.

As the person continues to sin, this bondage increases, and he reaches a point where it is extremely difficult—almost impossible—to use his agency. We can compare agency to a muscle. After an extended time of nonuse, the muscle atrophies. The basic muscle is still there, but the person has lost the ability or freedom to use it. That is how Satan brings us into bondage. Once we have given him enough of our freedoms, our agency becomes atrophied and we are in his power.

This is why repentance is so important. Once a wrong choice is made, our freedom to exercise agency is limited, and we must repent in order to remove that limitation. For instance, each time the girl chooses the immodest dress, she hinders her chances of returning to modest dress. Her physical and worldly motivations become stronger than the spiritual, until soon she is even uncomfortable in a modest dress. "Oh, that isn't me!" she will say, her self-image having been defined by her past choices. But her agency has not been taken away. At any time she could decide to change, though her freedom to make a change is hindered by shackles of habit and feelings that she has allowed Satan to place upon her.

Once our children understand the relationship between freedom and agency, we can teach them that to retain freedom a person must at all times accept responsibility for his own actions. Because consequences come later than the action, we may trick ourselves into believing that we can effortlessly slide through life and still progress. We think that we can get away with little sins or that we can manipulate and maneuver our way through life without paying attention to the laws—and without repenting. This is not possible, however, because whenever we break any commandment, no matter how small it may seem, we give up some of our freedom.

One young woman learned this the hard way. It was her freshman year at Brigham Young University and she was having trouble in school. Financial and emotional difficulties were pressing upon her. Faced with these and other problems, she worried and fretted, and instead of studying sought escape in the form of play. Naturally, she began doing poorly on tests. The realization that time was running out frightened her into reality, and she made appointments to talk with her teachers. But instead of admitting her mistakes and asking for help, she tried to avoid responsibility for her wrong behavior by telling "little white lies." The worrying had caused some minor physical problems such as headaches and stomachaches, so she exaggerated these maladies, blamed them for all the trouble she was in, and begged for leniency. All but one of her teachers gave her the benefit of the doubt.

After the talks with the teachers, she felt a great sense of relief and thought she could then start the next semester with a clean slate. She felt that she had avoided the consequences of her wrong behavior. But as time went by she realized that besides the financial and emotional problems, she now was suffering from guilt feelings (she had lost the freedom to have peace of mind), her self-esteem fell even lower (she had lost the freedom to like herself), and she realized she did not know the facts previously taught that were necessary to an understanding of the new material (she had lost the freedom to progress). Instead of avoiding consequences, she realized, she had brought on more consequences and was now in heavier bondage to her wrong choices.

At any point this chain of consequences could have been broken. If this young woman had accepted responsibility for her actions at the time of the interviews with her teachers, and then paid the price for her wrong behavior, the situation would have eventually reversed itself. She could have regained her freedoms. Even better, if she had examined the choice she was making when she chose to worry and play instead of study, the situation would never have evolved into a problem. She would have retained her freedoms.

The story has a happy ending in that the young woman learned a valuable lesson from the experience and resolved that she would pay the price of those past mistakes and accept responsibility for her future actions. She also learned that even if she tried to blame other people or circumstances, she would still have to suffer the consequences of wrong choices herself.

This brings us back to the quotation we started with: "There is no such thing as a lazy person, only a person who does not understand the principle of agency." As this young woman began to see how to use her agency, that she could choose through her actions the very feelings she would have, she began to take responsibility for herself and to grow in character and maturity.

Earning Privileges

The only way to stay out of Satan's power is to either make correct choices in the first place or to accept responsibility for wrong actions and repent. Repentance is the tool we use to break Satan's power over us. Even though the original moment of action is gone, repentance gives us the opportunity to right a wrong situation and to accept responsibility for what we have done.

To restate this in the positive: All privileges and freedoms must be earned—freedom to learn more in school, freedom to like oneself, freedom to be happy, freedom to establish good relationships, freedom to grow and progress, freedom to have the companionship of the Holy Ghost, and so on. As we earn these freedoms by making right choices, we become more like our Father in Heaven. However, if we make wrong choices and evade the responsibility of our actions, we become more like Satan. When we choose his ways, the only freedom we retain is the freedom to sin more.

As spiritually centered mothers it is important for us to understand this aspect of agency and use it with our children. We do this as we encourage and help our children to pay the price for the privileges they want in life by providing them with opportunities to earn privileges. This helps our children learn the relationship between paying a price and receiving the blessing.

In many areas of life we do this naturally and merely need to point out to the child what is happening. An example of this is when we teach our young children to show respect for others. The ways we show respect are called rules or manners, but as the child lives with the rules, an atmosphere grows which allows him the freedom to establish pleasant relationships with other people. If a child fails to follow these rules, the feelings generated inhibit good personal relationships.

In other cases we can teach this concept by making sure our children pay the price before we give them privileges. To do this, one father, instead of giving his son car keys as soon as he got a driver's license, set strict rules and also had his teenage son help pay expenses for the family car. When the son had proved himself, the father gave the boy his own set of keys.

One mother sets strict curfew rules for her children. As they grow older and consistently obey the rules, she explains that they have proved themselves by being obedient and have earned the freedom to set their own curfews. They then tell her what time they will be in at night. This is what maturing is all about. Maturity comes when a child lives within the rules until he has earned the freedoms or privileges. But when we give children freedoms and privileges before they have earned them, we allow traits of selfishness and self-indulgence to develop in the place of maturity.

Too often we mislead our youth. We give them awards they haven't earned, rationalizing that they would feel left out and be hurt if we didn't. When we do this we teach them that they don't have to obey the laws in order to reap the rewards. In an eternal sense, being given something one hasn't earned is more harmful than being left out, because the effects can keep people out of the celestial kingdom.

Sometimes we misteach by covering for a child's failures or misbehavior, thereby giving him the privilege of accomplishment without his having earned that privilege. This is one of the greatest detriments we can bring upon our children. Once in a while teachers or others who call problems to a parent's attention may be wrong or even vindictive, but most of the time they aren't. Denying that a problem exists or protecting the child by interfering with the consequences does no one any good, and often does the child great harm.

A friend once told me of a teenage boy who was fired from his job because he was caught drinking beer while at work. Instead of dealing with the problem, his mother went to the boss and demanded that the boy be given back his job. She even threatened a lawsuit if the employer didn't take the boy back. Over and over she kept saying, "My boy wouldn't do such a thing. He's never touched alcohol in his life. He's a good boy."

The employer had given the boy several chances and could see no reason to take him back, so the woman began legal proceedings. One week later the boy was killed in an automobile accident caused because he was driving while under the influence of alcohol.

Who is to say what might have occurred if the mother had not interfered with the consequences? Without her interference, would being fired have caused the boy to take a look at what he was doing to the exent of averting the tragedy? Had his mother's actions given him the false sense of security that she could cover for him in any situation?

The process of growing up will *always* entail some wrong choices and misbehavior. The significant thing is not how many problems we have in life, not how many mistakes we make, but how we handle the problems that do occur.

Recognizing the Reasoning Process

The next part of agency that we should teach a child is to recognize when he is using agency. Since agency is the power we have to protect ourselves against Satan, we must know how and when we are using it. As already stated, agency is a mental power, therefore, whenever we use it (other than as a habitual reaction) we go through a mental process called reasoning. We also reason when we use our freedom, but the questions we ask ourselves when we use agency will be different. When we find ourselves asking questions such as, "Should I or shouldn't I?" or "Does it really matter?" or "Once won't hurt, will it?"—questions that lead to "Is it right or wrong?"—we should recognize that we are about to use our agency.

It is interesting to read the story of Nephi and Laman and Lemuel and observe this reasoning process at work. When Lehi asked Laman and Lemuel to go back for the brass plates, they used their agency. They reasoned the request out in their minds and came to the conclusion that it was a hard thing Lehi required of them. (See 1 Nephi 3:5.)

Nephi also used his agency, reasoned the issue through, and said, "I will go and do the things which the Lord hath commanded, for I know that the Lord giveth no commandments unto the children of men, save he shall prepare a way for them that they may accomplish the thing which he commandeth them" (1 Nephi 3:7).

Reluctantly Laman and Lemuel did join Nephi and went back to Jerusalem. Laban, however, refused to give them the plates, and they left the city. After this an angel appeared to them commanding them to go back. The angel promised that the Lord would deliver Laban into their hands. But even after such a promise from an angel, Laman and Lemuel reasoned, "How is it possible that the Lord will deliver Laban into our hands? Behold, he is a mighty man, and he can command fifty, yea, even he can slay fifty; then why not us?" (1 Nephi 3:31.)

Nephi's answer was, "Let us go up again unto Jerusalem, and let us be faithful in keeping the commandments of the Lord; for behold he is mightier than all the earth, then why not mightier than Laban and his fifty, yea, or even than his tens of thousands?" (1 Nephi 4:1.)

Nephi, Laman, and Lemuel each reasoned through the available choices and came to a conclusion that determined his course of action. The difference was that Laman and Lemuel based their decisions upon the precepts and logic of men, while Nephi relied upon the teachings of the gospel, the promptings of the Spirit, and his faith in Jesus Christ. Basing a decision on this kind of rationale will always lead us to the ways of God. Basing a decision on the precepts of men will always lead us in the ways of men. Thus, by analyzing our thought processes in such instances we can always know, even before the action has occurred, what will be the consequence of the decision we are about to make.

But before we talk about these consequences, there is one more aspect of reasoning that must be explored. This reasoning process is easily recognized when we are attempting to make an important decision. But it is harder to recognize the process in situations that we call instinctive. For example: A child spills a gallon of milk in the refrigerator two seconds before the family is to leave for church. Without even thinking, the mother loses control and shouts, "Mary, how could you be so clumsy! If you'd be more careful! Look at the mess!" On and on she rants, or maybe she even grabs the girl and in her anger hits her. This mother didn't stop and reason what the right and wrong approach would be for that moment and decide to lose control. But we know agency was used because a choice between right and wrong was made. We also know that whenever agency is used there is a reasoning process. So where was the reasoning? In this case it came long before the action. At some point in time all of us decide, whether consciously or subconsciously, how we will deal with these types of situations.

Elder Richard L. Evans once said, "You cannot be something you have not become." Though there may be some exceptions (as in one afflicted with congenital or acquired nervous defects), normally a person who reacts with anger had to *become* a person who reacts with anger. At some point he had to choose to be that way. The decision may have been so far back in life that he does not remember it, and often the rationale was very subtle, such as, "This is how my parents deal with a situation so that's how I will deal with the same situations."

Every one of us has at one time or another said, "She makes me mad!" or "He made me do it!" In reality, however, no one makes us mad. We allow ourselves to become mad or angry or happy or sad. When we admit to ourselves that we choose our own feelings and actions, we have taken a major step of progression. Other people may provoke us, but they do not make us do or feel anything. As a child grasps this concept he begins to understand that he is indeed master of his own destiny.

Abraham's father was an idolator. He even allowed the priests to put Abraham on an altar for sacrifice to the pagan gods he worshipped. Yet Abraham became one of the great Old Testament prophets. How could this happen? Because he used this great power—agency.

We too can overcome our past or our circumstances. Agreed, it is often extremely difficult, but it is not impossible. Many people have done it before and many people will continue to use their agency to free themselves from bad habits and traditions and to make their earthly and eternal lives better.

To unlearn or change behavior we need to use our agency, reason through the choices, and choose to change. Then we need to follow through by determining a course of action that will help us change. For example, if anger is the problem we may decide to count to ten or to leave the room until our emotions are under control.

A friend of mine reeducates herself by writing notes and placing them all over her house so that she is constantly reminded and aware of the problem. These notes change as she masters or completes one reeducation process and begins another. They have included such things as, "I will talk in a soft voice to my children," "I will be cheerful when I wake up in the morning," and "I will eat only enough to sustain healthy life." These constant reminders are very helpful, especially if written in positive instead of negative statements.

We can think of many other helpful things to do if we just use our imaginations. One of my daughters was especially trying during her preschool years. She was into everything, on to everything, up to everything, and always two steps ahead of me. I've never met such a mischievous child! But my concern was mostly with my reactions to her behavior. She did these things out of curiosity at this great world she was discovering, and I was reacting as if she were a hired mobster. As I tried to decide what to do, I discovered that during these encounters I almost always used the phrase, "What am I going to do with you?" Acting on that discovery,

I drilled her until she would answer my question with the words, "Love me." After that, each time I discovered another mess, I'd immediately say, "What am I going to do with you?" When she'd look at me with those big blue eyes and answer, "Love me," what else could I do?

These same principles of changing behavior apply to our children. We should help them learn ways to change behavior, and encourage them to be constantly growing and progressing.

Spiritual Blessings

Now let us go back and examine more fully the topic of reasoning and consequences. When we base our decisions upon the teachings of the gospel and the promptings of the Spirit, the most significant consequence is that our faith increases. King Benjamin said that the Lord "doth require that ye should do as he hath commanded you; for which if ye do, *he doth immediately bless you*" (Mosiah 2:24; emphasis added). One of the immediate blessings is increased faith, and it is only by obedience that we gain faith. Elder Bruce R. McConkie tells us: "Faith is a gift of God bestowed as a reward for personal righteousness. It is always given when righteousness is present, and the greater the measure of obedience to God's laws the greater will be the endowment of faith." (*Mormon Doctrine* [Salt Lake City: Bookcraft, 1966], page 264.)

An LDS woman once told me that one cup of coffee wouldn't hurt her. "It takes many cups for the caffeine to harm you," she said, and she may have been right. I doubt that one cup of coffee will hurt her physically, but even half a cup will hurt her spiritually because drinking coffee after having been commanded not to is an action of disbelief and rebellion.

In the sight of God, all the laws he gives us are spiritual. (D&C 29:35.) Naturally, then, spiritual benefits or consequences come from living those laws. Too often we expect temporal blessings to come when we live spiritual laws; then if they don't, we doubt the laws. For instance, we experience times when we suffer health problems or financial reversals or other difficulties even though we are living the commandments. It is tempting then to say that blessings do not follow obedience. In these circumstances we need to remember that it is necessary to be tried and tested, and sometimes the waiting experience is part of this. Temporal blessings for obedience will at some time be given, but it is the spiritual blessings that come immediately on compliance with the law.

Besides increased faith, these spiritual blessings include joy, happiness, peace of mind, love, self-esteem, and every spiritual gift. If we stress these consequences of right choices instead of always dwelling on the consequences of wrong choices, or on temporal consequences, we help motivate our children to righteous living.

Before we talk about how to teach our children of consequences, we need to discuss how important this concept of faith development is to us as mothers. As we come to understand how spiritual blessings—especially faith—are gained, we can better assist the development of faith in our children. When we realize that agency is the key to the acquiring of faith, we also understand why no one, including our children, can be forced to accept the gospel. That was Satan's proposed way, which we fought against in the premortal world. No one can be permanently compelled to righteousness or obedience. In order to gain faith, the faith that is necessary for continued righteousness, a child must use his own agency to choose to do what is right. If he is only doing right because a parent or a teacher is compelling him, he gains no faith because he has not used his agency. In order to gain faith each child must be free to choose, have a knowledge of the truth to base his choices upon, and then come to value that truth.

In many areas of a child's life we go through this faith-building process without even realizing what we are doing. For example, we kneel with a young child, and word for word guide his prayers. In this way we teach him or give him knowledge. As he grows older we listen each night as he prays. Then we remove ourselves from the situation, leaving him free to choose. He then prays not because we are standing there waiting for him to do so, but because he chooses to pray. Eventually his own experiences with prayer teach him the value of that eternal principle.

When we understand this process, we can spend our time and energies teaching and setting the example instead of trying to force righteousness upon our children. Our primary purpose as spiritually centered mothers is to educate the consciences of our children. We do this by teaching correct principles such as honesty, tithing, obedience, love, and chastity. We teach these things both by word and by example, and also by making sure that our children are at meetings and other places where the things we are teaching in the home will be reinforced by others. Then, as our children practice and experience gospel principles operating in their lives, they will come to love and value truth.

Teaching About Consequences

When teaching our children about the spiritual blessings and consequences of choices we can read them stories such as those of Laman, Lemuel, and Nephi, and share teachings such as Alma's sermon on the seed of faith (see Alma 32). This can be done for younger children by using visual aids and analogies they will understand. We can also point out incidents of reasoning, faith development, and consequences that are found in these stories. Examples from our own lives or the child's life also help teach these things.

Another way to teach this process of reasoning, of choosing to be obedient and gaining faith, is to compare it to using our muscles to lift weights. The more we exercise the muscle, the stronger the muscle becomes, therefore it becomes easier to lift the weights and we can in fact lift heavier ones. It is the same with our agency. By choosing to be obedient we increase our faith. The more faith we have, the easier it is to be obedient. I draw a circle for the children so they can see the concept as I explain it.

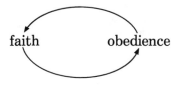

faith   obedience

Brigham Young said, "When faith springs up in the heart, good works will follow, and good works will increase that pure faith within them" (*Discourses of Brigham Young* [Salt Lake City: Deseret Book, 1954], page 156).

I have also found it very helpful to use the following chart to trace the potential courses our choices lead us along. The chart shows the spiritual consequences that follow a decision, and helps make the process more visual for children. For older children I use the whole chart. For the younger children, I simplify it by only using the italicized parts and by omitting the scriptures.

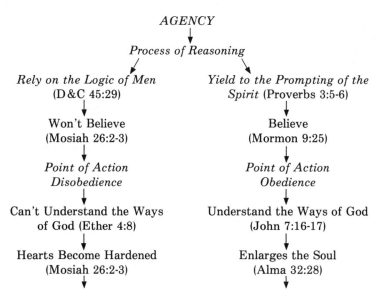

AGENCY

Process of Reasoning

Rely on the Logic of Men (D&C 45:29)	*Yield to the Prompting of the Spirit* (Proverbs 3:5-6)
Won't Believe (Mosiah 26:2-3)	Believe (Mormon 9:25)
Point of Action Disobedience	*Point of Action Obedience*
Can't Understand the Ways of God (Ether 4:8)	Understand the Ways of God (John 7:16-17)
Hearts Become Hardened (Mosiah 26:2-3)	Enlarges the Soul (Alma 32:28)

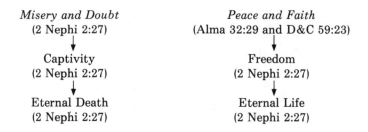

Misery and Doubt	*Peace and Faith*
(2 Nephi 2:27)	(Alma 32:29 and D&C 59:23)
↓	↓
Captivity	Freedom
(2 Nephi 2:27)	(2 Nephi 2:27)
↓	↓
Eternal Death	Eternal Life
(2 Nephi 2:27)	(2 Nephi 2:27)

We can also teach the law of consequences with examples from the physical world. When we run into a chair we get a bump or bruise. When we touch a hot stove we get burned. After learning that the stove is hot, we don't keep touching it. We learn from the experience, treat the wound until it is healed, and then avoid repeating the incident. After discussing these things, we can compare them to the spiritual laws and commandments by explaining that when we tell a lie or steal or break any commandment we hurt our spiritual selves. In order to heal these spiritual wounds we must repent and avoid further injury by refraining from the sin.

Another effective method for teaching consequences is to "talk choices" with a child. After contemplating the possible choices, talk through each one and examine what the consequence of each will likely be. By "talking choices" we mean just that. It isn't a time for preaching, unless we want the child to just shut us out. The most effective way to talk is to ask questions and let the child respond. The right answers don't often come on the child's first response, especially at first use of this method. But a series of questions usually brings him to the point where he recognizes for himself and puts into his own words the things we want him to learn. Only when we see that he doesn't know the answer should we tell him.

I was doing this with Breana and Talena when they were five and seven years old. I asked each to name some of the consequences of fighting with her sister. They gave me several good answers, such as: we aren't happy, we don't love each other as much, we hurt each other's feelings, we lose the peaceful feelings within us, my sisters don't respect me as much.

They named a few more, but still hadn't said what I wanted so I finally added, "And when we fight, the Holy Ghost can't dwell with us."

Talena's eyes opened wide in astonishment as she exclaimed, "No wonder you don't want us to fight!"

I won't pretend that this approach ends fighting overnight, but it does make the child stop and think about what he is doing. Coupled with other measures, this contributes to the cause of family harmony.

Any of the problems we are having with our children can *at the appropriate time* be put in question form and analyzed in terms of consequences. Again, this doesn't immediately solve the problem, but it helps the child understand that all behavior elicits a consequence. Some children and even adults never realize that they pay a price or a consequence for their choices. But the consequences come as surely as night follows day, whether we recognize them or not.

The stress on "at the appropriate time" is important. Success in talking through situations is dependent upon having these talks at the right time. Few, if any, teachings sink in when tempers or emotions are high. Teaching moments come at peaceful times when the Spirit is there to help us communicate. One mother told me that when tempers flared or when heated conversation started she would remove herself from the "battle" by refusing to yell or argue back—if need be even leaving the room. Later, when she was calm and collected, she would either initiate a conversation that could be constructive or write a letter to the child.

With smaller children, and in some situations even older children, another way to teach reasoning and consequences is in the form of a game. Present a situation and then ask the child first for a negative reaction and then for a positive reaction. For example, you might say, "You have just come home from school. You go into your bedroom and find that your little sister has gotten into your drawers and messed everything up." Then you have the child respond with a possible negative reaction and a possible positive reaction. If the mood is right you can discuss the feelings each response would generate within the child, in the little sister, and in yourself. Sometimes to avoid any possibility of negative reinforcement we should ask only for positive reactions.

Another effective method is to stop an experience at a crucial point and simply ask, "How do you feel inside right now?" Again, it takes a little practice to get the right timing, but this works for positive or negative situations and helps the child to recognize the feelings his actions generate within himself. Sometimes in the negative situations, however, the child stubbornly responds that he feels good when you know he doesn't. Nothing need be said. The experience still makes him think about the way he feels, even if he refuses to give you the right answer.

Another good learning activity when a wrong choice has been made is to ask the child to tell you what he could have done differently that would have made the situation turn out better.

The hardest part of teaching consequences is that often the natural consequences of our actions don't appear for many years. A bright child who will not study or apply himself in school might still get good grades and not experience the natural consequences of what he has given up until he is out of school. It might be twelve or thirteen or more years before he realizes the price he has paid by his lack of study. He has lost the freedom of being able to call upon stored knowledge for the answers to many of life's problems. He has not learned how to concentrate. He lacks the character and maturity that hard work bring. He lacks the discipline and self-mastery that come from living up to one's full potential.

To help solve this problem, we as mothers can affix immediate consequences to many of our children's actions to teach them responsibility and to help them avoid the more severe long-range consequences. For example: We can set consequences for not studying or for irresponsible behavior that will encourage the child to study and to behave. Missing a meal, losing privileges, or doing extra chores can be affixed consequences for misbehavior. Likewise, consequences can be set for good behavior. If a child gets his work done fast and efficiently you can explain that because the work was done so well and so fast it has given you a little extra time. Then ask the child how he would like to spend the next twenty minutes with you. There is a lot written and said about affixing consequences to bad behavior, but it is just as important to link consequences with good behavior. It is often so easy to let good behavior go unrecognized that I have found I must constantly remind myself to remember the good. Such simple things as a thank-you note, a special hug, praise, or even just a special look and wink can be consequences for good behavior.

In other cases consequences are natural, and as mothers our job is simply to allow them to happen. A while back I realized that I was interfering with natural consequences and causing myself a great deal of frustration. I had taken upon myself the responsibility for waking up the family every morning. I'd go into each room and shake them, call to them, beg them, sing to them, but couldn't get them up in time. It was ruining my mornings. Then I began to realize that getting up was their responsibility, not mine. They were becoming self-indulgent because I was not allowing them to be responsible for themselves. Realizing this, I bought everyone alarm clocks and gave them the responsibility for getting themselves up. I also made a rule that if anyone missed prayer they had to do the breakfast dishes. Some mornings I get a little worried and have to restrain myself from interfering, but as the children have suffered a few consequences they have learned to accept responsibility for themselves.

Another thing that occurred to me only after I started applying these principles was that true guilt is a great tool of the Lord. (True guilt is a by-product of sin and should be distinguished from, for example, the frustrations we sometimes feel at not being able to do all we'd like to do.) Usually when enough guilt feelings are built up in us, we repent. Guilt is a healthy thing if we allow it to prod us on to repentance. It also serves as a kind of moral thermometer. When we feel guilt feelings, just as when we feel a fever, we know something is wrong. It is time to retrace our steps, figure out what we have done wrong, and correct it. Psychologists today often try to cure problems by taking away the guilt instead of changing the behavior that caused the guilt. This is like taking an aspirin for a toothache. It doesn't cure the problem, but only masks it. In the long run it also hurts rather than helps the patient because the tooth continues to decay.

My first experience with this concept was very profound. I had fixed one of my daughters a tuna-fish sandwich for lunch. She was five years old at the time and disliked tuna fish and practically everything else. I gave her the sandwich explaining that she could have dessert as soon as it was eaten. Then I left the room. About three seconds later she came bounding out of the kitchen exclaiming that she'd eaten the sandwich and wanted dessert. I knew she hadn't had time to eat the whole thing, but I walked back into the kitchen with her. Sure enough, the sandwich was gone and I had a good idea where it was. Normally I would have found the sandwich, lectured her on the virtues of nutrition and honesty, and demanded that she eat. Instead I looked right into her big blue eyes and said, "You know what is right and you know what is wrong." Then I left the room.

I went down the hall expecting the usual arguments and accusations, but instead there was silence. I waited a few minutes until curiosity got the best of me. Walking back down the hall, I stole a look as I passed the kitchen door. There, sitting Indian-style on the floor, was my five-year-old, eating her sandwich right out of the garbage can.

As I analyzed this experience I realized that too many times I have alleviated my children's guilt by inflicting a punishment upon them. My tongue-lashings are a punishment and in essence have stifled or erased guilt feelings. My children feel entitled to the sin because they have paid the price or suffered the punishment for it. By restraining myself on that occasion and leaving the burden of responsibility upon my daughter, I allowed her conscience to prod her to do what I had been unable to make her do on countless other occasions.

As we use the various methods of teaching consequences, our children will come to learn about agency, how it works, what we should be using our agency for, and the consequences that happen when we use agency. At this point we should teach that we can best use our agency at one time: We do this by making a commitment to *always* do what is right. Then when we come to a moral choice, we don't have to stop, reason, and decide. We just decide once that from that point on we will do what the Lord wants. We will follow the promptings of the Spirit and obey the commandments.

John 6:38 gives the Savior's words, "For I came down from heaven, not to do mine own will, but the will of him that sent me." (See also D&C 19:24.) This is the secret as to why the Master could be perfect. He did his Father's will at all times. No doubt, this did not always mean that the Savior received a direct, specific revelation as to what the Father would have him do; rather, having committed his agency to God, he applied it to principles and circumstances to make the right moral and spiritual choices, and that, of course, resulted in his doing the Father's will. Basically, that is how we do the Father's will in any particular today. The Savior did it in *all* particulars.

As we guide our children to use their agency to try the ways of the Lord and to live the commandments, they will gain their own testimonies. We are told, "If any man will do his will, he shall know of the doctrine, whether it be of God, or whether I speak of myself" (John 7:17).

Summing Up

To help our children learn to use their agency, we must:

1. teach our children what agency is and of its importance to their personal salvation.
2. teach our children to recognize by their reasoning process when they are using agency.
3. teach our children that every time they use their agency a consequence will occur, and what the spiritual consequences are.
4. understand how agency builds faith in order to help the process of faith development and to avoid hindering or stopping the process.
5. teach our children the commandments and help them to value the eternal truths.
6. help our children commit to using their agency to always do what is right.

Chapter 5

Step Four: Learning About the Savior's Mission

> *"Look unto me in every thought; doubt not, fear not. Behold the wounds which pierced my side, and also the prints of the nails in my hands and feet; be faithful, keep my commandments, and ye shall inherit the kingdom of heaven."—D&C 6:36-37*

A few years ago when our family was reading the New Testament together, I was very discouraged. We were about halfway through the book when I began wondering if anything was even getting through to the younger children, and if perhaps it was a waste of time to include them. Then one morning I heard six-year-old Breana marching up and down the hall repeating in her best sing-song fashion, "Verily, verily, I say unto you. Verily, verily, I say unto you."

A tickle went up my spine as I realized that she was listening after all. If she picked that up, she was also learning other things. Even if all she was learning was the rhythm, sounds, and beauty of biblical language, that was a start. Taking heart from this, we went on with scripture study, even on mornings when everything seemed not only pointless but hopeless.

On the surface the story might seem humorous and somewhat insignificant, but another reason that tickle went up my spine was that those words, "Verily, verily, I say unto you," were the key to my testimony that the Book of Mormon is true. Those words are often used in the New Testament, always by Jesus himself. When I first read the New Testament I came to recognize those words as a phrase the Savior used to emphasize what he was about to say.

My own father ends almost every other sentence with, "You know what I mean." Every time he says it I get a little smile inside of me and think, "That's my dad!"

As I read the New Testament the same thing happens. I hear those words, "Verily, verily, I say unto you," and a warm smile of recognition passes through me.

After I made this discovery, I was reading in Third Nephi about the Savior's visit to the Book of Mormon people. As I read his words to them I again heard, "Verily, verily, I say unto you." A warm, delicate feeling trickled through me, then swelled to a marvelous crescendo. This was a different book, a different continent, a different time, but the same Jesus Christ. This was the same man I had read about and come to know in the New Testament.

It is a small thing, but it was the beginning of my coming to know my Savior. I hope that it will also be a beginning for Breana—a very important beginning that every child, every person, must make.

Looking to the Savior

As spiritually centered mothers we have the great responsibility to help our children come to know Jesus Christ, to make him real to them, to teach them to look to him in faith.

Joseph Smith once had a vision in which "He saw the Twelve going forth, and they appeared to be in a far distant land. After some time they unexpectedly met together, apparently in great tribulation, their clothes all ragged, and their knees and feet sore. They formed into a circle, and all stood with their eyes fixed upon the ground. The Savior appeared and stood in their midst and wept over them, and wanted to show Himself to them, but they did not discover Him." (Orson F. Whitney, *Life of Heber C. Kimball* [Salt Lake City: Bookcraft, 1967], page 93.)

In Numbers 21:7-9 we are told that fiery serpents went among the children of Israel biting the people and causing many to die. The people, hardened in iniquity, begged Moses to take the serpents away. Moses took the problem to the Lord and was instructed to make a pole with a fiery serpent atop, raise the pole in the camp, and have the people who were bitten look at the serpent in order to be healed. The story continues in the Book of Mormon when Nephi tells us, "because of the simpleness of the way, or the easiness of it, there were many who perished" (1 Nephi 17:41).

Keeping any and all of the commandments will turn our hearts to the Father and his Son, but scripture study, fasting, partaking of the sacrament and prayer are especially important commandments for accomplishing this. However, these things seem such simplistic answers to modern life's complex problems that often we, like the children of Israel, deny ourselves the blessings available. Our Savior has already given his very life for us. He desires to help us, to comfort us, and to guide us. He is in our midst waiting for us, longing for us to lift our eyes to him. But we, like the Twelve in Joseph's vision, like the children of Israel, must look to him to receive his help. We must knock, we must seek, we must ask. We must invite the Savior into our lives, come to know him, and help our children to do the same.

Gaining and sharing knowledge about the Savior's mission constitute the fourth teaching step. In many ways this can be accomplished in the same manner as learning and teaching about our Heavenly Father, for the Father and Son are one in principles, powers, and perfections. One of the teaching methods we talked about in chapter 3 is especially important: that is, to make the Savior part of our homes, or more specifically, part of our daily living.

Many homes display pictures of Jesus to serve as constant reminders of him to family members and all who pass through. There are a number of beautiful pictures of the Savior with little children that are especially nice for children's rooms. Not only do these pictures serve as reminders, but they are springboards to many conversations and teaching moments. They reinforce such general concepts as how much Jesus loves little children, but can also illustrate more specifically his love for each individual.

Many mothers tell of bringing their families closer to the Savior by trying to always act as if he were right there. This is a difficult thing to do, but, as with most difficult tasks, trying and falling short is a great improvement over never trying. We can help ourselves accomplish this challenge by remembering that it is not really a case of *pretending* that the Lord is there or that he knows what is happening. He does know what we do and what we say. Rather than pretend he is there, we should make ourselves constantly conscious of the fact that he knows and sees all, and then we should act accordingly. In turn, we can help our children to always feel the Savior's presence in their lives.

In coming to know the Savior, as with learning of Heavenly Father, it is helpful to learn of his nature, character, and attributes. Joseph Smith taught: "Three things are necessary in order that any rational and intelligent being may exercise faith in God unto life and salvation. First, the idea that he actually exists. Secondly, a correct idea of his character, perfections, and attributes. Thirdly, an actual knowledge that the course of life which he is pursuing is according to his will. For without an acquaintance with these three important facts, the faith of every rational being must be imperfect and unproductive; but with this understanding it can become perfect and fruitful, abounding in righteousness, unto the praise and glory of God the Father, and the Lord Jesus Christ." (*Lectures on Faith* [Salt Lake City: N. B. Lundwall], page 33.)

Children can also be helped to more fully understand Jesus by being taught of his premortal role. Young people love to hear the story of their Brother who stood at the great council in heaven as Heavenly Father discussed his plan for our salvation. "And the Lord said: Whom shall I send? And one answered like unto the Son of Man: Here am I, send me. And another answered and said: Here am I, send me. And the Lord said: I will send the first." (Abraham 3:27.)

Children are interested in the conflict that ensued as Satan rebelled and Jesus boldly stated, "Father, thy will be done, and the glory be thine forever" (Moses 4:2). It is a powerful story with which children can easily identify. They even understand that Satan was using the very thing he wanted to take away from all of us: agency.

This was the beginning of opposition as recorded in our scriptures. It is pleasantly surprising that the thing children have the most trouble understanding is why one-third of the hosts of heaven would even follow Satan.

Teaching About Satan

A discussion of this premortal experience also provides a good opportunity to teach about Satan. Children need to know that he is real and has power. They should know what Satan is like and what motivates him. Jesus loves us and seeks to strengthen us, to exalt us, to make us as he is, to lead us to the Father. Satan wishes to devour us, to drag us down to his level of misery and damnation. (See 1 Peter 5:6-8.) Satan is extremely selfish. One reason he even bothers with us is to get us to worship him, to give to him more followers. In almost all aspects Jesus Christ and Satan are opposites of each other.

When Satan appeared to Moses, "Satan cried with a loud voice, and ranted upon the earth, and commanded, saying: I am the Only Begotten, worship me" (Moses 1:19; see also verse 22). In this verse we see Satan's personality revealed.

He is the father of all lies, evil, cunning, wicked, full of anger and hatred, and is driven by passions and desires. Jesus is full of truth, goodness, wisdom, righteousness, discipline, and love. Whenever he has appeared to men, instead of begging them to worship him, as Satan does, he teaches, instructs, and offers the most glorious gifts that could ever be bestowed, the truths of the gospel. Jesus Christ is a giver; he gave his very life for us. Satan is a taker.

While it is never good to dwell on Satan or his powers—too much of that drives the Spirit away and invites Satan into our presence—we can help our children to distinguish the good from the evil and to know where each comes from by teaching them of Satan.

The Attributes of Jesus

To further build a child's love for the Savior, we teach of the birth of Jesus. He was literally the Son of God, both in body and spirit. This allowed him to triumph over death because of the immortal traits he inherited from his Father, and at the same time to experience the joys, pain, and frustrations of mortality because of the mortal traits he inherited from his mother.

More than anything, reading and telling the stories of Jesus' life and ministry will bring our children closer to him. They can discover through these stories the marvelous traits Jesus possesses. The stories never grow old and every child has a favorite he wants to hear over and over again. Most children are especially captivated by the story of twelve-year-old Jesus in the temple. (See Luke 2:40-52.) As they read and hear these stories, they also come to understand that he experienced the same feelings and emotions they have experienced. Many of the stories point out how fatigued Jesus became from the hours of preaching and being pressed upon by the multitudes of people, but *always* he put other people's needs before his own. As our children understand this, they will come to feel that he can and will do the same for them.

All scripture in some way testifies of the Lord, so by reading any of it with our children we guide them to him, but chapter seventeen of Third Nephi is especially powerful in teaching of the Savior's love, compassion, and tenderness, and of his mission. Almost every verse in that chapter can be enlarged upon and discussed with children. As we read these and other scriptures and tell the stories of Jesus at bedtime, home evenings, and as we travel, we make them part of the children's lives. As we do this, however, we should stress that, unlike fairy tales, these stories really happened. Jesus grew from grace to grace because of the things he experienced. He was real. He lived upon the earth in the meridian of time and lives still in an exalted state.

Sometimes because of our own limited understanding we tend to rationalize away the Savior's perfections. We tend to give him human failings from our own frame of reference. For instance, when we do something wrong we tend to think that Jesus does not love us because we have sinned. We as human beings tend to make our love conditional, therefore, we think that the Savior does the same. At other times we ascribe to him the human failing of impatience or think that he doesn't understand us and our situations. None of these failings belongs to the Savior. Like God the Father, he has unconditional love for us. He accepts each man on the level he is on and offers the help necessary for that person to climb to a higher level.

In all our teachings concerning the Savior we should stress that Jesus loves and cares for each individual. He should never be portrayed as a harsh taskmaster, nor should we convey the idea that the Savior is displeased with the child. Jesus might not approve of a child's actions, but he would never disapprove of the child. We must be careful to distinguish between the two.

In the New Testament we are told that at the beginning of his ministry Jesus fasted for forty days and then was sorely tempted and tormented by Satan. He knew it was possible to fast for many days. Yet later while he was preaching to the multitudes he said to his disciples, "I have compassion on the multitude, because they have now been with me three days, and have nothing to eat: And if I send them away fasting to their own houses, they will faint by the way" (Mark 8:2-3).

We might have said in our impatient way, "Three days isn't that long to fast. People can and have gone much longer than that!" But the Savior understood the level the people were on, and having love and compassion for them he fed them. They didn't ask him for food, but he perceived their need and provided food.

We must not try to bring the Lord down to our understanding. Instead we must bring our understanding up to a true realization of the Savior's perfections. This also means that we do not try to establish a human kind of familiarity with him. He is the Savior, the Master, our Lord—and in our quest to know and follow him we must reverently acknowledge who he is.

We also encounter problems when we only bring up the Savior in negative situations by saying such things as, "Jesus doesn't want us to do that." We may mean well, but by so doing we associate the Savior with negative feelings and experiences. To accomplish the opposite we can highlight pleasant situations when everyone is feeling good, maybe working congenially together or sharing something special, by commenting, "This is how the Savior wants us to feel all of the time."

Sometimes that sparks more conversation; at other times the subjects move on. But the point is made and the children associate the Master with the good they are feeling at the moment. There are many other ways we can make these associations and teach the nature of the Savior if we just look for the opportunities and use a little imagination.

In addition to this, we should vocally express our love for the Savior in front of our children. Our children need to hear us express our testimonies and to know that we do love and have faith in Jesus. This should happen not only in formal testimony meetings but in family settings such as home evenings, and in personal conversations.

The Atonement

As a child's love for the Savior begins to take root and to blossom, as he comes to understand the character and attributes of the Savior, we can teach of the fall of Adam and Eve and how the atonement of Jesus Christ makes resurrection and eternal life possible. Jesus was the only sinless person to ever live. If he had not been free from sin he could not have atoned for our sins. He gave the ultimate sacrifice, his life, so that we could return to God. That fact in and of itself is enough to show his love for us.

One example that helps young children understand the Atonement is to explain that because of the fall of Adam it was as if all of us except Jesus were locked in a prison. He, being perfect, was not put in prison, and since he was not in prison he had the opportunity to obtain a key that would open our prison door. In order to open the door, however, he had to die, to give up his own life to obtain possession of the key. Because he loved us so much he did suffer and die, he did obtain the key, and he did open our prison door. We by our righteous living must now walk out of the prison and follow the Savior to our Heavenly Father.

Elder Boyd K. Packer's classic example using the gloved hand (see *Ensign*, July 1973, page 51), has deeply implanted in my children the meaning of resurrection. Carl first used the example with them at home evening. He explained to them the difference between spirit (comparing it to his hand) and body (comparing it to the glove). Then he slipped his hand into the glove as he told them about birth. After a little discussion about life, he took the glove off and explained how the body and spirit separate at death. Then he talked about Jesus and how he had made the Resurrection possible. As he spoke he put the glove back on his hand. This is a powerful object lesson and also helps to prepare a child to understand and accept death when it happens to someone close to him.

Relating the sacrament and the sacrament prayers (see D&C 20:77, 79) to the Resurrection and the Atonement also helps teach the meaning of these events. Jesus gave and blessed the first sacrament and instructed his disciples to partake of it often, that they might remember his body which was crucified for them and his blood which was shed for their sins. The sacrament is to remind us of the Resurrection and the Atonement—that it is only because of Jesus Christ that either is possible. By meditating and concentrating on these things during the time the sacrament is being passed, we draw close to Jesus and gain great power and strength that enable us to live more righteously. We should always partake of the sacrament worthily and use the time not only to think about the Savior, but to recommit our lives to him. It is a time to determine to overcome sins and shortcomings and to focus our attentions and intentions on the Savior.

This is, however, hard to accomplish while juggling a one-year-old and a two-year-old on your lap and trying to stop the seven-year-old from tickling the five-year-old who is disturbing the elderly lady in front of you. But as mothers we can accomplish the same feeling of closeness to the Savior if, while holding the children, we concentrate on how much we love them, generating Christlike thoughts and feelings within ourselves. He knows what we are going through and wants to help us. If we give up, saying, "It's impossible; I'll wait until the children are grown," we miss out on the blessings. But if we generate these Christlike feelings during the sacrament, he will recognize the intents of our hearts and bless us with the same spiritual power and peace in our lives as when we are able to meditate without distraction.

Part of explaining about the Atonement and resurrection is teaching that resurrection will be for all mankind, but the Atonement will only be fully beneficial to those who repent and forsake their sins. In order for the Atonement to help us, we must follow the teachings of the gospel and live the commandments, or we must suffer ourselves for what we have done wrong. Referring back to the analogy of the prison, this means we must repent or the Savior cannot use his key to get us out. (See D&C 19:15-19.)

Repentance

As we teach of repentance we need to be careful not to convey it as a negative experience. Repentance is a beautiful growth process, and as such it should be part of every single day for us and our children. Repentance is the means by which we grow and better ourselves, the means whereby we break Satan's hold over us. Therefore, it is valuable to help our children learn how to repent.

We can divide the process of repentance into five steps. First, we recognize our wrongdoings and desire to overcome them. Second, we confess our wrongdoings to our Father in Heaven in prayer, to the person or persons we have wronged, and sometimes to our bishop, depending on the seriousness and nature of the offense. Third, we make restitution if possible for what we have done wrong. Fourth, we forsake our wrongdoings. Fifth, we forget our wrongdoings and move forward in the service of the Lord. Once we repent, we must not dwell on past sins and let them spoil the future.

Each step is important. True repentance cannot happen if even one of the steps is omitted. If we—carefully and with the proper attitude of love—guide a child through each step when he has done something wrong, explaining and teaching as we go, the beautiful feeling of joy that repentance brings will be his. This feeling will serve as reinforcement and motivation and will help a child to further progress.

We must be careful when dealing with small children, however, that we don't label as sin harmless imaginations or mistakes. In young children fantasy and dreaming play a vital role in development. While we need to help a child distinguish between reality and fantasy, it would be unwise to eliminate, or worse still to make him feel guilty for, pretending. During the first few years of his life we should guide and direct and lovingly help him to distinguish between reality and fantasy, good and evil. After this has been accomplished we can teach repentance with love and understanding.

Baptism

Teaching our children the meaning and importance of baptism is also part of this step. Telling the story of Jesus' baptism is a good way to introduce the subject. (See Matthew 3:13-17.) This is one of the few places in scripture where we have all three members of the Godhead physically represented at one time: Jesus Christ being baptized, God the Father's voice proclaiming his Son, and the Holy Ghost descending like a dove. We can explain to our children what an important occasion God must have considered it for him to reveal all three of the Godhead at once.

To reinforce the teachings of baptism I have found it helpful to make each child's baptism a looked-forward-to and sacred experience. With our first child this was a little harder to do than it has been with the others. But since the baptism of the oldest, the younger girls have remembered her experience and looked forward to their baptism days with great anticipation.

Our girls only have birthday parties on their odd-numbered years: five, seven, nine, and so on. This leaves the eighth birthday without distraction so that we can stress the spiritual without confusion and excitement of other things. Very early on the morning of her baptism, Carl takes the child someplace where the two of them are relatively alone. Two of the girls went to the mountains to watch the sun come up, and talked about what a special day it was and about what would be happening. Two others chose to go to the visitor's center on Temple Square where similar conversations took place. Each child asks any questions she might have and Dad reviews exactly what he will do in performing the ordinance and why. Then the two of them go out to breakfast together. Two or three months previous to this he also takes the child to witness a baptism.

Besides things such as these you can tell the children about your own baptism and how special it was. You can read about baptism from Mosiah 18:8-13, going over each item talked about in verse nine and discussing how they as individuals can accomplish it. Some children are even able to discuss Doctrine and Covenants 128:12, in which Joseph Smith teaches us the symbolic significance of baptism.

The most important thing, however, is that each child knows that through baptism we enter the kingdom of Jesus Christ and actually take his name upon us, and that by taking his name upon us we become eligible for many eternal blessings. (See Mosiah 5:8-9.)

Carl was the bishop when Laresa and Talena were baptized, so they had the unusual privilege of being interviewed by their father. With our third and fourth daughters, Breana and Anissa, it was also special to have someone outside the family stressing and reinforcing through a personal interview the things we had taught. We try to make this appointment as important as possible by dressing up for it and talking about it before and after.

To further stress and accentuate the importance of baptism we have also made it a tradition that each member of the family treats the others on the anniversary of his or her baptism. The treat is a simple one, such as cookies or donuts, but gathering to enjoy it gives us an opportunity to talk about the person's baptism and the importance of baptism. A person's baptism day, endowment day, and marriage day are three of the most important days of his mortality. As we celebrate each child's baptism day, it gives us the opportunity not only to honor the importance of that day, but to talk about the other two days that the children will experience.

Preparing for the Second Coming

Another aspect to consider when teaching of the Savior is the importance of preparing our children for the Savior's second coming. When the Lord lived on the earth in the meridian of time he descended below all things and triumphed. When he comes again, he will be over all things, ruling the saints in power and glory. It will be a beautiful time, a time we should look forward to with excitement and anticipation. Doctrine and Covenants 49:22-25 and 133:42-49 contain important basic information about the Second Coming. These and other verses will help us prepare our children so they will recognize the advent of the Savior's coming. Here again, however, we must find the happy medium in our teaching.

If we or our children do not first have a testimony of the love and personality of Jesus Christ, these things that are meant to prepare us may be frightening. If we wait to explain these things until the child's love and knowledge of the Savior are firm, then the concepts will not be terrifying, but exciting. At times we must stress the love, joy, and excitement that will attend the Second Coming, and teach that for those who are righteous it will be a glorious occasion. It will be a great and dreadful day: great for the righteous who are prepared, and dreadful for the wicked who are not.

The best way to teach of the events of the Second Coming is to first study and learn about these things ourselves. If we know the signs predicted in the scriptures so we can distinguish between prophecy and the rumors that sometimes circulate—if we have a feeling for the Second Coming—we can judge what each child needs to know. But the basic fact that Jesus Christ will come again in love and glory and power to dwell with the righteous can be taught to every child.

Feelings About the Savior

While all the things we have talked about are very important in teaching about the Savior, it is hard if not impossible to convey in writing the *feelings* we must try to instill in a child's heart so that he can come to know the Savior and the Father. While we must do all we can to make these feelings a part of the child's heart, still we need to understand that we cannot just give these feelings to our children.

If I have a friend I want you to know, I might tell you all about her. I could describe how she looks so well that you would recognize her. I could tell you about her life and personality. You might even come to feel as if you know her yourself, but until you meet her and begin sharing experiences with her she is still my friend and not yours.

There are two important things to be learned from this example. One is that in order for us to introduce our children to the Savior we must first gain a testimony of the reality and importance of his mission. Only by coming to know him ourselves, through service and study and obedience to his commandments, will we be able to introduce our children to him. The second thing we learn is that after the intellectual and informative things we teach, it will be the feelings about Christ, the love and light the children experience as they obey his words, that will make him real to them. As King Benjamin said, "For how knoweth a man the master whom he has not served, and who is a stranger unto him, and is far from the thoughts and intents of his heart?" (Mosiah 5:13.)

As spiritually centered mothers we have the task of leading our children to the Savior so that the Savior can lead them to God the Father. We must set the foundation and prepare the way, or the spiritual experiences that bring testimony will go unnoticed or misunderstood.

Becoming Sons and Daughters of Christ

Volumes can and have been written about the Savior and his mission. These few pages do not begin to cover the many aspects of the duties that are his as he carries out our Father's plan. The few things discussed here are only a beginning for us to use as the foundation that our children can build upon. As they grow older and begin to study and learn more, they will come to understand how we, by being born again, can become the sons and daughters of Christ. "And now, because of the covenant which ye have made ye shall be called the children of Christ, his sons, and his daughters; for behold, this day he hath spiritually begotten you; for ye say that your hearts are changed through faith on his name; therefore, ye are born of him and have become his sons and his daughters" (Mosiah 5:7).

In simplest terms, being born again, or becoming sons and daughters of Christ, comes by being obedient to the things Jesus taught. As children grow older and begin to study the gospel themselves, they will come to understand more fully what this means, if we have previously laid a foundation by teaching them about the Savior.

In the last chapter we talked about obedience as it relates to faith. We should note here that the attitudes we assume while being obedient are very important. In order for obedience to build faith, we must be exercising it in order to glorify God the Father, not to accomplish selfish desires of fame or fortune. Our motives and intentions must be pure or our actions avail us nothing. We must keep the commandments because we love the Father and his Son, not because we want glory or approval from those around us. We must serve because we want to further God's work, not because we want to further our own ends. We also obey to show our love for Heavenly Father and the Savior.

Centering Holidays Around Jesus

One final thing I have found helpful in teaching about the Savior is to consciously center Easter and Christmas celebrations around him. To start each of these holidays we pop corn and make other treats, then get comfortable in the dining room and read the story of the Nativity or the Crucifixion. As we read we tape poster-size pictures to the wall at the children's eye level. These pictures illustrate the story we are reading. For weeks before Christmas and Easter these pictures are a constant reminder of the true meaning of the holidays, and they set the mood for our celebration.

We also take time to discuss the symbols of Christmas and Easter that are part of the world's celebration of these events. Some of the symbols, such as stars, are obvious. Others are not so obvious: the evergreen tree representing everlasting life, the red of the poinsettia symbolizing the blood Jesus shed for our sins, or Easter eggs representing new life made possible by the Atonement. Looking for and discussing these symbols moves our minds in the right direction and fixes spiritual meanings to the things the children see throughout the holidays.

As we make Jesus Christ a part of our lives and the lives of our children, all aspects of those lives become better, including the destination—for "it shall come to pass that whosoever shall believe on the Son of God, the same shall have everlasting life" (Helaman 14:8).

Summing Up

In order to teach the mission of the Savior we must:
1. teach the correct character and attributes of Jesus Christ.

2. teach the character and nature of Satan.
3. teach the Resurrection and the Atonement.
4. teach the importance of baptism.
5. teach the importance of repentance and how it is accomplished.
6. bring the Savior into our homes so as to make him a part of each day and a reality to each child.

Chapter 6

Step Five: Inviting the Spirit into Our Lives

> *"But the Comforter, which is the Holy Ghost, whom the Father will send in my name, he shall teach you all things, and bring all things to your remembrance, whatsoever I have said unto you."—John 14:26*

A man once went to his bishop very distraught over the relationship he had with his son. The boy had never gained a testimony of the gospel, and as he grew older he had begun to rebel against his parents and the Church. Every time the father tried to help the boy, it ended in terrible fights and arguments. Now the son was about to leave home.

As the father poured out the sorrows of his heart, the bishop felt impressed with the fact that neither he nor the parents could convert the boy. The only one who can convert anyone is the Holy Ghost. So he advised the man to fast and pray until he *knew* the Spirit was with him, and then take the boy camping.

"Just the two of us?" The father was surprised.

"Yes," the bishop answered. "Go someplace where you can be alone with your son."

"But we can't even be in the same room without fighting! What would I say to him? What would I do with him all alone?"

"That's easy," the bishop answered. "Don't do anything or say anything unless the Spirit prompts you to."

The father humbly accepted the advice. He fasted, prayed, and studied the scriptures until he *knew* the Spirit was with him; then he took the boy camping. Neither said a word as they traveled the winding mountain roads to the canyon campground and found a beautiful campsite nestled in the quaking aspens. They ate in silence, then rolled their sleeping bags out under the stars—still without conversation. As they crawled into their bags they exchanged a few polite comments about the beautiful night, the stars, the canyon, but nothing more. The minutes seemed like hollow hours as they lay in the expansive darkness. The father worried, wondered, but feeling no promptings to question or teach he remained silent. Long, awkward moments passed. Each knew the other was awake, but still no one spoke.

After some time, slow, quiet sobs from the boy broke the stillness. Little by little he began to speak. He asked for forgiveness, explained how wrong he had been about his father, and expressed a desire to be given another chance, promising he would be different. The father hadn't said a word, yet for both the father and son it was an unforgettable moment as they exchanged feelings spirit to spirit; feelings that proved strong enough to change a young man's life.

No parent could have caused such a turnabout himself, but when we teach by the Spirit, communicate by the Spirit, the humanly impossible becomes possible. Lives change. Love and truth are communicated and become the foundation for our teaching.

A Spiritual Environment

As this man learned, we cannot convert our children. That is the function of the Holy Ghost. But there are many things we can do to prepare the way for the Spirit. One of these is to create a pleasant physical environment that is conducive to the Spirit.

I had the opportunity once of visiting in the home of a branch president in a little town near Mexico City. The kitchen had no running water, only a small table and four chairs, a fire to cook on, and a bare electric light bulb illuminating the room. Yet there was a special feeling there. The room was clean. The bare cement floor was spotless and the walls were clean. Colorfully painted dishes lined the open shelves and there was a sense of order in the small area. Even though poor, the good wife had created an environment in which special warmth and goodness could grow and thrive— an atmosphere that welcomed the Spirit.

I had another friend who had this type of home also. It was nice, although not elegant by the world's standards. The colors were soothing, the rooms neat and clean, and it was obvious that every attempt had been made within budget to make the house comfortable and inviting. But the beautiful feeling I got when in that home went beyond these physical things. Finally I was so curious I had to ask what caused that warm, special feeling. My friend replied, "When we moved into this home my husband gave it a special priesthood blessing that it would always be a place where the Spirit could abide. Since then we have done everything possible to make that blessing a reality."

These women had each created a special physical and spiritual environment that had far-reaching benefits.

In Moses 1:18, Moses said to Satan, "I will not cease to call upon God, I have other things to inquire of him: for his glory has been upon me, wherefore I can judge between him and thee. Depart hence, Satan."

If children are raised in a home that has a special spiritual feeling about it, they will, like Moses, be better able to feel the difference between good and evil. They will be comfortable with good, while evil places and evil feelings will be uncomfortable to them.

A friend once told of going to a used book shop to sell some old books. As she entered the store she was overcome with unexplainable dark feelings. She looked around, but could see nothing to justify the feelings. Hurriedly she conducted her business and literally raced to get out of the place, unable to abide the feelings a minute longer. Later she discovered that the store was a front for pornographic materials. She had seen nothing, but she had felt the evil influences.

In our quest for spiritually centered motherhood we can benefit by spending more time preparing to obtain and keep the Holy Ghost with us and less time trying every psychological gimmick that comes along. This doesn't mean that we discount the helps that psychologists have given us. The gospel teaches us to use all the truths provided us, including our own common sense and wisdom. We can study and use the things behavioral scientists have learned, but instead of blindly trying every new idea we should let the Spirit guide us as to how and when to use the techniques we learn from these other sources. By letting the Spirit direct us as to what to do and when to do it, we can succeed.

The Nature of the Holy Ghost

As with other members of the Godhead, it is important that we first understand the Holy Ghost's nature, mission, and character and teach these things to our children. The Holy Ghost is the third member of the Godhead. Because of this he is one with the Father and Jesus Christ in principle and purpose. He differs from them, however, in that he does not have a physical body, but is a personage of spirit. Many of the names he is called by in the scriptures identify him thus: Spirit, Spirit of God, Spirit of the Lord, Spirit of Truth, Comforter, Holy Spirit of Promise—all are titles for the Holy Ghost.

In understanding the Holy Ghost we should note that the personage of the Holy Ghost can be in only one place at a time, but his influence can penetrate to all places or persons at a time.

One way to explain this to children is to liken the Holy Ghost to the sun. There is only one sun, yet millions of people at one time are warmed by its rays, and its light permeates into the very corners of our homes. The influence of the Holy Ghost works in much the same way. It is also an interesting analogy that on a cloudy, rainy day the sun is still shining, but clouds keep us from receiving the full benefits of its warmth and light. Likewise our sins and shortcomings become clouds that keep us from receiving the blessings and benefits the Spirit would like to give us.

To help illustrate this I put on our dining-room bulletin board a large sun and ten figures to represent the members of our family. I explained the concept of the Holy Ghost being like the sun and then I put a cloud between the sun and the people and made the analogy of the cloud being sin. After the discussion, I left the illustration on the bulletin board. When Grandma and Grandpa visited, the girls got to explain the analogy to them and on other occasions to friends who were curious.

It is the primary mission of the Holy Ghost to testify of God the Father and Jesus Christ. (See 3 Nephi 28:11.) The Holy Ghost is also given to us to be a comfort and guide in our lives. I had often heard of and experienced the power of the Holy Ghost as a guide, but it was only a few years ago that I first came to know the Holy Ghost as a comforter. Our daughter Talena had been admitted into the hospital for a routine tonsillectomy. She went in Sunday afternoon and was to be operated on Monday morning, but early that morning the doctor told us that her blood would not clot properly. Under these circumstances he could not operate. Hurriedly he made an appointment for us to see a hematologist, released her from the hospital, and sent us home.

I managed to maintain a great front while Talena was with me, but as soon as we got home and I was alone, I went to pieces. My mind throbbed with horrid possibilities. I cried, I worried, I feared the very worst. Then finally, still alone in the den, I knelt down and poured out my heart to my Father. I begged that Talena would be all right, that she would be healed. For a long time, and with tears still flowing, I prayed. Finally I listened. I waited for what I wanted to hear, that she would be healed, but nothing came. So I prayed again, and as I did the most marvelous feeling enveloped me from the tip of my toes to every hair on my head. Words cannot adequately describe the feeling: a feeling of intense love, a magnificent, engulfing feeling of comfort and peace. I was given no answer, but the worry, the fear, the torment were completely erased from my mind and heart. I knew that whatever happened it would be the Lord's will, that he loved me and would sustain me.

Through the next two months as they repeatedly tested Talena, not only didn't I worry, but I couldn't worry. One by one the tests came back negative, yet her blood was still not clotting properly. The hematologist couldn't explain the problem even after all the testing was repeated, but still I could not worry or fear. Finally it was decided that we should wait and see what happened. Two years later another test was taken and the problem had disappeared. Talena is healthy and growing and I was spared ulcers!

The Holy Ghost is our friend, a true friend who desires the very best for us: celestial life. He will do all in his power, and that power is great, to help us achieve that goal. As the other members of the Godhead do, the Holy Ghost understands our trials and tribulations and why they are given to us. He understands our problems, our desires, our hurts, our frustrations — but more, he knows our mission in life, our full potential, and our ultimate destination. Knowing and understanding these things, the Holy Ghost, if we will let him, will guide and direct us. "For behold, again I say unto you that if ye will enter in by the way, and receive the Holy Ghost, *it will show unto you all things what ye should do"* (2 Nephi 32:5; emphasis added).

Gaining the companionship of the Holy Ghost and then abiding by the promptings of the Spirit is the single most important thing we can do to become spiritually centered mothers. It is also the most important thing we can teach our children to do. They need to know what they should do to receive the Holy Ghost and how to live by the promptings of the Spirit. We cannot be with them every moment to help them in their decisions and trials, but the Holy Ghost can. If we make our children dependent upon us we will fail, but if we teach them to be dependent upon their Father in Heaven, Jesus Christ, and the influence and guidance of the Holy Ghost, they can be helped at any time, at any place, in any situation, according to their needs.

The Gift of the Holy Ghost

To lead our children to this point we can help them understand that the *gift* of the Holy Ghost is not synonymous with the Holy Ghost. Many people assume that when they are confirmed they then have the Holy Ghost with them at all times. This is not necessarily so. A good example that helps teach this concept to children is to compare receiving the gift of the Holy Ghost to putting a telephone in our home. The telephone is there to use, but if we don't lift up the receiver and dial when we need something we don't get any service out of the telephone. When it rings, if we don't answer we never get the message. It is possible to have a telephone in our home and never use it—never answer the ring, never make a call.

So it is with the Holy Ghost. The gift of the Holy Ghost is the privilege to have access at any time to the promptings and guidance of the Spirit. It is like having a telephone installed in our home. But in order to have the Spirit with us we must use it and be worthy of it. To receive the Spirit into our lives, we must take the necessary steps to pick up the receiver and listen. These steps include: 1. Being baptized and confirmed; 2. Fasting and praying for the companionship of the Spirit (see D&C 19:38 and 42:14); 3. Living and thinking righteously, repenting when necessary; and 4. Studying the scriptures.

The Promptings of the Spirit

After teaching our children how they may obtain the companionship of the Spirit, we can teach them how to recognize the promptings of the Spirit. Sometimes the Holy Ghost puts words, exact words, into our minds. (See Helaman 5:45-47.) At other times he places feelings in our hearts and minds that direct and guide us.

After Oliver Cowdery tried to translate but failed in his attempt, the Lord explained: "Behold, you have not understood; you have supposed that I would give it unto you, when you took no thought save it was to ask me. But, behold, I say unto you, that you must study it out in your mind; then you must ask me if it be right, and if it is right I will cause that your bosom shall burn within you; therefore, you shall feel that it is right. But if it be not right you shall receive no such feelings, but you shall have a stupor of thought that shall cause you to forget the thing which is wrong; therefore, you cannot write that which is sacred save it be given you from me." (D&C 9:7-9.)

Learning to recognize how the Spirit prompts and speaks to us is an individual effort. No one can describe it exactly. But if we practice this procedure in dealing with our day-to-day problems, we will be able to recognize and trust in the Spirit to guide us in our big decisions and problems.

In teaching her children this procedure, one mother writes a note of love and encouragement in the front of a triple combination which she and her husband present to a child on his eighth birthday. In the note the child is challenged to live by the advice given in Doctrine and Covenants 9:7-9, which she underlined in red before giving the child the book.

Solving Problems

In learning to reason out decisions to present to the Lord, we need to know how to attack problems. Too often we recognize that a problem exists, but feel helpless as to what to do about it. There are, however, a few problem-solving skills that will help us.

First, identify the cause of the problem. An experience occurred with my oldest daughter that really brought the importance of this step home to me. She came home from church one Sunday in a very bad mood, and as the week progressed so did her bad humor. The baffling thing was that there had been no incident in our home to spark this type of reaction. I tried pouring on love and I tried being firm, but the behavior continued. I tried several times to get her to tell me what was wrong, but she wouldn't. Finally after much patient coaxing I got her to open up to me. "Last Sunday we had a Young Women's meeting," she said, "and the speaker showed us all the advertisements the Church has on TV." She stopped then, and mumbled awkwardly that I wouldn't understand and that she didn't want to hurt my feelings, but finally she went on. "Well, those commercials tell all about how parents are supposed to be, and you're not like that."

I was amazed! My good relationship with my daughter had been shattered by the Church's TV "commercials"! I could have struggled for years and never guessed the cause of her distress. But after identifying the cause we were able to solve the problem by simply discussing it. Her problem was with an ad that sent the basic message: when a child comes home a parent should drop everything and give undivided attention to the child. I explained that the mother in the ad was watching television, an activity that she could drop, but that often when my daughter came home I was busy with another child. I went on to explain that as a mother of eight children I have to choose priorities. Sometimes I choose wrong, but usually I am working on the most important things for that moment, and I hope that in the long run it will all work out even and fair. Then I reassured her that despite my imperfections I loved her very much. That was enough. She accepted my explanation and reverted back to her good-natured self.

Very often we fail with our children because of this one thing: We don't stop to determine the cause of problems. A child may be doing poorly in school, but is it because he needs glasses, is afraid of the teacher, has missed a basic concept so that now he is lost, daydreams instead of listening, or just doesn't care? A child may tease the life out of a sibling, but is it because of jealousy, stress he is trying to vent, feelings of inadequacy and low self-esteem, because he wants our attention, or because someone else bullied him earlier in the day? Just trying to stop the teasing or fighting will not stop the problem.

This process of analyzing problems becomes easier if we pray for guidance. Sometimes we will be told or made to know through our feelings the cause of the problem. Other times, as with Oliver Cowdery, we must study it out in our minds and then ask the Lord if we have correctly identified the problem.

Second, after identifying the cause of a problem we should prayerfully decide how we are going to solve the problem. In searching for solutions we should be creative, let our minds explore. The ideas that come first, that seem obvious, aren't always right. It is also sometimes good to seek advice from trusted and knowledgeable people or ones who have faced similar problems. After thinking through the possibilities, perhaps even writing them down, we should decide which solution would be best. It is this solution that we take to our Heavenly Father in prayer, asking if it is right.

If after approaching the Lord in prayer we do not receive a burning within or a stupor of thought, we should examine our lives to see if we have anything we need to repent of in order to be worthy of an answer. If we don't, we can either assume that this is a decision our Heavenly Father wants us to make alone, that either solution would be all right, or that we must wait longer for the answer.

We do not need to wait until a child is eight before teaching him this process. While it is true that a child does not receive the gift of the Holy Ghost until he is eight, prior to that time each child, every person in the world, can be guided by the light of Christ. (See D&C 84:45-47.)

It is the light of Christ that teaches men good from evil; that is its function. The world calls this influence conscience. Even our small children are directed by the light of Christ, and by teaching them to examine and recognize their feelings—to really listen to and obey those deep inner feelings— we prepare the way for them to receive and be guided by the Holy Ghost.

We can encourage this listening habit by not making every decision for our children. When a child comes to you and asks, "Is it all right to play baseball with my friends on Sunday?" You can ask him to honestly examine his own feelings, the promptings within himself, and if need be to pray about it and then decide for himself.

When doing this we must remember that some of the greatest learning experiences happen when a child lets peer pressure or personal want override his inner feelings. It often takes patience on our part, and sometimes courage not to worry about what the neighbors may think, but the turmoil and inner struggles a child suffers from a bad decision can teach him much. The important thing is that we first educate the conscience by teaching correct principles and then rely upon the Holy Ghost to direct us as to when and what we should do in these instances.

The Spirit as Teacher

As mothers we should also prepare the way and then trust more in the Holy Ghost to teach our children. At a sacrament meeting a speaker addressed several valuable insights and comments to the teenagers in the audience. Repeatedly during the talk one mother turned to her son and whispered as she poked him in the ribs, "Listen to that. That's what I've been trying to tell you. That's what you should do."

Her motives were pure, but if the Spirit were going to bear witness to the boy, prompt him, or help him in any way, she was making it impossible for him to hear or receive the message.

It is perhaps the hardest thing we need to do, but if instead of always preaching, always trying to force principles and teachings upon our children, we would spend more time inviting the Spirit into our lives and our homes, we would be more successful. The Spirit can teach our children things we never can—and what is taught by the Spirit is long remembered, while what is preached by a parent is often forgotten. This is why it is so important to have the Spirit with us as we teach.

I have never had such a frustrating, discouraging time as when I have tried to teach the principles of the gospel without the Spirit. I have learned that when this happens, when something is wrong in my life so that the Spirit is not with me, I might as well save my words. At these times I have to review, repent, and pray until I am ready. Then and only then can I really teach. It is impossible to communicate the things of the Spirit without the presence or influence of that Spirit. But when the Spirit is present, fantastic things happen.

When our children were younger, December was such a hectic, demanding month that by Christmas day I was usually drained both physically and emotionally. In order to "recharge my battery" I would reserve the day after

Christmas for myself. On that day the children were involved with friends and new playthings, and we could subsist on Christmas leftovers.

One particular year I had decided that I would spend "my day" reading the Doctrine and Covenants. The morning of the appointed day came and I snuggled into the den couch and began with section 1. I stopped only to feed the family, and by the end of the day I was filled to overflowing with joy and the Spirit. To spend an entire day with the scriptures was a fantastic experience. But at the end of the day I wasn't through with the reading and it was such a wonderful experience that I decided to take part of the next day and finish.

The next morning I picked up where I had ended the day before. It was even more wonderful. My mind seemed to explode with knowledge and my heart pulsed to new heights of joy and love. But two unsupervised days proved to be too much for the children. By the afternoon of that second day they were quarreling and contending. I could hear them in the other room and my heart ached. While I was experiencing a spiritual feast, they were a few feet away fighting! At first I thought they could work it out, but as the screams and shouts got louder I knew I had to intervene. Stalking into the family room, the words, lectures, and accusations that I normally used when upset filled my mind. But when I opened my mouth to speak, the words wouldn't come out. I was amazed! I could feel the words on my tongue, hear them spinning in my head, but I could not utter the awful words.

As I stood there awkwardly, my mouth open, the children stared dumbfoundedly. At that point I did the only thing I could: I fell to my knees, threw my arms around them, and told them how much I loved them. The Spirit communicated with them. Love did what anger never could; the fighting stopped.

I wish I could say that this has happened every day since then, but I can't. I get caught up in day-to-day living and forget. When this happens to any of us we need to review and repent and bring ourselves back to where we were. But each time we do this we learn a little more; each time it gets a little better, and by trying instead of giving up, we can be assured that we are *slowly* becoming better persons.

Gifts of the Spirit

Another important function of the Holy Ghost is to bless us with the gifts of the Spirit. We should teach our children to seek after these gifts in order to perform their missions in life. Wisdom, knowledge, healing power, discernment, speaking in tongues, and prophecy are just a few of these great gifts. (See 1 Corinthians 12:4, 7-11 and D&C 46:11-33.)

In Doctrine and Covenants 46:11 we are taught, "For all have not every gift given unto them; for there are many gifts, and *to every man is given a gift by the Spirit of God.*" We, along with our children, need to seek and obtain these gifts in order to do the Lord's work while in mortality. Paul counseled, "Follow after charity, and *desire spiritual gifts*" (1 Corinthians 14:1).

These gifts can be a great source of strength and power in our lives and the lives of our children, but we must seek them out and develop them through use and practice if they are to benefit us and others. (A good story that helps teach this is the parable of the talents found in Matthew 25.)

Seeking after the Spirit is the greatest endeavor we can undertake. It enhances every area of our lives. Parley P. Pratt said: "The gift of the Holy Ghost...expands, and purifies all the natural passions and affections, and adapts them, by the gift of wisdom, to their lawful use.... It develops beauty of person, form, and features. It tends to health, vigor, animation, and social feeling. It invigorates all the faculties of the physical and intellectual man. It strengthens and gives tone to the nerves. In short, it is, as it were, marrow to the bone, joy to the heart, light to the eyes, music to the ears, and life to the whole being." (*Key to the Science of Theology,* 1978 ed. [Salt Lake City: Deseret Book], page 61.)

After coming to understand the Holy Ghost and the immense help he can be in guiding us to become spiritually centered mothers, it is interesting to ponder several questions. What impact would it have on an unborn child if during the nine months of gestation the mother had the constant companionship of the Holy Ghost? What teaching could take place in the years before a child learns to speak if we used the Spirit? What foundations of love, security, and self-esteem could we give our infants and young ones by communicating with them through the Spirit?

Yielding to the Spirit

King Benjamin instructed his people, "For the natural man is an enemy to God, and has been from the fall of Adam, and will be, forever and ever, unless he *yields to the enticings of the Holy Spirit,* and putteth off the natural man" (Mosiah 3:19; emphasis added).

Brigham Young explained how to yield to the enticings of the Spirit: "When you are overtaken in a fault, or commit an overt act unthinkingly; when you are full of evil passion, and wish to yield to it, then stop and let the spirit, which God has put into your tabernacles, take the lead. If you do that, I will promise that you will overcome all evil, and obtain eternal lives." (*Discourses of Brigham Young,* page 70.)

I like to compare this to shifting gears in a car. If you try to shift straight from reverse to first gear you strip the gears. Likewise, it is next to impossible to change directly from a negative emotion to a positive one. Emotions are too strong. But if instead we just concentrate on moving the negative emotion to "neutral," or in other words stop the negative actions and feelings until we have control enough to think and reason, then we can follow the promptings within us and move to the positive emotion. In neutral we can gain the help of the Spirit that is necessary to move to the positive.

Brigham Young explained the beautiful consequences that can come after we have learned how to do this. "When through the Gospel, the Spirit in man has so subdued the flesh that he can live without wilful transgression, the Spirit of God unites with his spirit, they become congenial companions, and the mind and will of the Creator is thus transmitted to the creature." (*Journal of Discourses* 9:288.) It is at this point that the Holy Ghost becomes our constant companion.

Summing Up

To teach our children of the Holy Ghost, we must:
1. create an environment where the Spirit can dwell.
2. teach our children who the Holy Ghost is and what he does.
3. teach our children how to obtain the Spirit for themselves.
4. teach our children how to study out their problems and how to present possible solutions to the Lord in order to receive answers.
5. teach our children to seek after and develop the gifts of the Spirit.
6. teach our children to yield to the promptings of the Spirit and to depend upon the Spirit for guidance and direction.

Chapter 7

Step Six: Living the Law of Consecration

"And they did walk uprightly before God, imparting to one another both temporally and spiritually according to their needs and their wants."—Mosiah 18:29

A tiny acorn holds within its shell the possibility of becoming a huge, beautiful tree. A seed the size of a salt grain has potential to grow into a life-sustaining vegetable or a delicate flower. The world is filled with many kinds of seeds, each containing the possibility of something bigger, something greater, something more valuable.

We, too, carry within us potential that is far bigger, far greater, than any of us can now comprehend. Parley P. Pratt said: "An intelligent being, in the image of God, possesses every organ, attribute, sense, sympathy, affection that is possessed by God himself. But these are possessed by man, in his rudimental state, in a subordinate sense of the word. Or, in other words, these attributes are in embryo and are to be gradually developed." (*Key to the Science of Theology*, page 61.)

My heart races every time I read that quotation. Just think, within us is every attribute of godhood! All we have to do is nourish those traits, feed them, enable them to grow. In this way, just as the seed does, we attain our full potential and become like our Heavenly Father.

Mortal life is a training ground, a preparatory school for godhood. The gospel as contained in the scriptures and words of the prophets is the curriculum. But to activate the knowledge we gain, to assure that this knowledge is fed and nurtured in order to begin the process of change that is necessary for us to become gods, we must live the laws of obedience and consecration.

The Principle of Consecration

Often we talk about consecration only in terms of imparting of our material goods to the poor and needy. Or we think of the United Order as something we will someday be required to live, and in this way dismiss the law of consecration as a sometime-I-will-have-to-do-it thing. But consecration takes place here and now, and it entails much more than the giving or sharing of material goods. Consecration means to set our hearts upon righteousness and to put the things of God first in our lives. The law of consecration includes giving of one's time, talents, and strength to the building of God's kingdom.

The law of consecration is a law of great power and spiritual strength. It is also a principle that, when correctly lived, brings joy to the soul and peace to the mind. As with all of God's laws, the blessings and rewards of living the law of consecration far surpass any of the earthly sacrifices we might make to live it.

To lay a foundation for the teaching of consecration to our children, we should help them understand that everything they have and are is a gift from God. One of the ways we teach this is by making it a point to thank our Father in prayer for the things we have been given. Taking nature walks while we discuss the creation of the earth, or acknowledging who gave us the beautiful world, also impresses the source of all blessings on a child's mind. Other times just a comment in passing, such as, "I'm thankful Heavenly Father sent you to me," or, "I'm so happy Heavenly Father gave me eyes to see," can serve as a reminder and reinforce the fact that everything good comes from God.

As our children begin to understand who gave us all things, we then can teach that no matter how hard we serve, how much we give, we will always be indebted to God for these blessings. All that we have, he has given us. We in turn have a responsibility to use our gifts, talents, and blessings to help build the kingdom of God here upon the earth. We do this by serving others. As King Benjamin explained, "When ye are in the service of your fellow beings ye are only in the service of your God" (Mosiah 2:17).

In Jacob 2:18-19 we are told, "But before ye seek for riches, seek ye for the kingdom of God. And after ye have obtained a hope in Christ ye shall obtain riches, if ye seek them; and ye will seek them for the intent to do good—to clothe the naked, and to feed the hungry, and to liberate the captive, and administer relief to the sick and the afflicted."

As the scriptures instruct, the most important goal to instill in our children is that of seeking after Jesus Christ and God the Father. Then they should better themselves, increase their talents, earn a good livelihood, learn, and in all ways increase their own capacities so that they have more to give and more to share with their fellowman.

Learning to Work

This brings us to the point that a prerequisite to living the law of consecration is hard work. There is no shortcut to the personal and material accumulation of something worthwhile to share. Work is the only honorable way to do it. By teaching our young children early in life to enjoy work, we make this step easier.

The Lord told Adam, "Cursed shall be the ground *for thy sake*" (Moses 4:23; emphasis added). Work is indeed for our sakes. From work we gain physical stamina, knowledge, self-discipline, self-esteem, and countless other blessings. Even the youngest of children can be given simple chores to do, such as clearing the table or unloading silverware from the dishwasher or drying and putting silverware away. I have noticed that in performing small tasks our young children feel more like part of the family, more like members of the team. Their self-esteem is improved by the feelings of accomplishment, and they learn the value of helping. This doesn't mean that they don't have lapses of self-pity: "Why do I have to do it?" But overall the cumulative experience adds up to the fact that they are learning to work and the blessings are being recognized.

Developing Talents

Another part of our task as spiritually centered mothers is to help our children discover what special talents, abilities, and gifts they have that can be shared with others. Musical, artistic, or writing talents can all bring as much joy to those in need as money or material gifts. An ability to organize, to tune a car engine, to type, to tell a joke, to make things grow, or to express love is often more needed than the monetary gift. We should encourage our children in any such areas in which they show interest and talent.

We need to seek the guidance of the Spirit to help us discover these special abilities and talents. We can also encourage our children to pray and seek for this same guidance. After an ability is recognized, we should do all in our power to help nurture and develop the gift.

There are many books and articles available on how to use games and charts to make chores and practicing more interesting to children, so we won't go into this here. However, we must recognize that it is important to be careful and selective when using these approaches. My own experience has been that no one method works for very long, and that new games must be used periodically. Also, while many gimmicks work for a while, I feel that in the end they may teach a child to do right things for the wrong reasons and prevent the child from feeling the joy that is the natural reward for what he is doing. If we are aware of this pitfall, however, we can help the child make the transfer to doing right things for right reasons. Getting a child to accept the responsibility of work without all the gimmicks takes longer and requires more patience, but the results are worth it.

The best help I have found is to follow the guidelines set forth in chapter 4 on agency. Overall, children work better if we set the rules and let them know what is expected, let them know the consequences of inadequate performance, and let their consciences guide them. For this to work, however, we should not step into their areas of stewardship and thus free them of the responsibility by taking it upon ourselves.

A few years ago I was attempting to give my two oldest daughters piano lessons. I set up a schedule and assigned them each a lesson time. Week after week the appointed time would arrive and they had not practiced. I became very frustrated. I nagged. That didn't work. I made charts with little stars to record practice time. That didn't work. I rewarded when they practiced. That didn't work. I prodded and pleaded and praised good work. I tried everything and nothing worked!

Then I realized that I was assuming the responsibility for their practicing. At that point I decided to back off. "When you've practiced enough that you feel good about your pieces," I told them, "come and get me and I'll give you a lesson." Now the responsibility was theirs.

At first they didn't respond. It was as if I had freed them from jail! But I held my ground and didn't say a word. Then, after the initial shock, they began to play on their own. Before long I was giving them lessons two and three times a week instead of once. Instead of being a pain, the lessons were the reward.

Consecration Through Service

As we learn to fix responsibility and our children begin to develop talents and to learn to work, we can then help them to use their abilities to serve their fellowmen. This is one of our primary purposes in life.

This was taught to me forcefully on one occasion. I spent the first several years of my married life in a pattern of living wherein I would give my family and husband all of myself. I'd serve, work, please, and then all of a sudden start to feel sorry for myself, going into a period of intense selfishness. "Who's trying to please me? Who cares about my needs? Who's serving me?" I'd complain to myself.

Then the festering selfishness would begin to hurt enough that it would prod me to turn things around, and once more I'd serve, work, and please. One day while in the selfish swing of the cycle I began to cry to myself, "Who cares what I like or what I want? While I spend all my time waiting on a thankless husband and ornery kids, who is going to do something for me? When am I going to have time to make myself happy?"

Just then the distinct feeling—admonition, rather—came over me, "You weren't sent to earth to make yourself happy, but to make others happy." (I would later discover that this was only part of the story—that it was by making others happy that my own happiness would be secured.)

This was a turning point in my life. Since then I have come to realize that previously even when I was serving my family I was doing it for selfish reasons.

King Benjamin said, "I would that ye should impart of your substance to the poor, every man according to that which he hath, such as feeding the hungry, clothing the naked, visiting the sick and administering to their relief, both spiritually and temporally, according to their wants" (Mosiah 4:26).

There are several key issues concerning consecration contained in these few words. 1. Every man should impart according to what he has to give. 2. We should administer to both the spiritual and temporal needs of others. 3. We should give according to others' wants—not the selfish wants but the largely non-material essentials to the person's well-being.

Gifts of Self

Imparting to others according to what we have is a very important concept. In the New Testament we are told that Peter and John were on their way to the temple to pray when they encountered a man lame from birth who asked them for money. Peter answered, "Silver and gold have I none; but such as I have give I thee: In the name of Jesus Christ of Nazareth rise up and walk" (Acts 3:6).

Peter probably did not have the money asked for, but such as he had, he gave—and how much better it was than money! Often we are so caught up in thinking about what we don't have that we overlook what we do have. And, as with Peter, often what we do have is a much greater gift than what we are worried about not having. Sometimes we can give food or clothing or money, but at other times we can give a smile, love, friendship, a song, a prayer, or our testimony. There is no one who has nothing to give others!

Consecration becomes a part of every day as we realize this and start to ask ourselves such questions as, What do I have that the Lord would have me share with this person? For what purpose did our paths cross at this time? How can this person's life be better or happier for having encountered me? The answers to these questions are not usually money or clothing or food, but as with Peter it is the things that we have within us, such as faith, that we need to give. If our children are taught early in life to think of these things, their lives will be not only more productive but happier.

Material Gifts

We have been talking mainly about the nonmaterial parts of consecration, but the material gift is also important when that is what is needed. As a matter of fact, to try to give the spiritual gifts to people who are physically hungry is next to impossible. Teaching our children to share of their material means is best done (as is all other teaching) through example. We can involve our children in the preparation of food to take to the sick. We can also encourage children to prepare things for their friends who are sick. Two young brothers in our ward brought our daughter a box of Popsicles when she had her tonsils removed. It was a special uplift for ailing Talena, and caused me to think a lot about the great lesson their mother was helping her sons learn.

On occasion, when my husband was bishop, families would bring cakes or cookies with notes telling him how much they appreciated him. It was amazing how these people always seemed to come just when he needed the encouragement most.

One family in our ward made it a home evening event to take a treat each week to another family. Each family member took a turn choosing the family that would be treated. A note was attached to the treat explaining that it was from the Family Night Phantom. The recipient was instructed to in turn make an anonymous treat for another family and deliver it the next week with the same message attached. The family would place the treat on a doorstep, ring the bell, and disappear before the door was answered.

In our family we draw names on the first of March, and from then until St. Patrick's Day we have secret leprechauns. Each family member that is old enough concentrates on doing and giving things to the person whose name she has drawn. All this is done in secret until St. Patrick's Day when the leprechaun makes herself known to the person she has been helping. This has become a fun annual event that we all look forward to as much as Valentine's or Thanksgiving Day.

Gifts of Time

Another way we can help our young people learn of the law of consecration is by encouraging them to share their time. Time is a gift all of us can give. We can encourage our children to babysit without pay for young parents while those parents are doing church work. We can encourage them to assist widows or elderly people with odd jobs or to perform other acts of service.

In ways such as these, we develop in our children a desire to do things for others. It makes doing good fun and exciting. Children are able to actually experience the joy of giving and sharing.

Tithes and Offerings

We also teach the law of consecration when we teach our children to pay tithes and offerings. We should explain what these monies are used for and encourage our children to participate. Our children had an opportunity to donate to the building fund for the Jordan River Temple, and ever since then Talena has said that because she helped build it, she wants to be married there. This is not something we drilled into her, but something that came from inside her as a result of her giving. We have had similar experiences as our children have donated to chapel building funds. A great sense of partnership and belonging is fostered, not to mention the faith, testimony, and love the children gain as they sacrifice for these projects.

Proper Attitudes in Giving

In teaching the law of consecration we must also be careful to instill in our children the proper attitudes. Consecration involves wanting to help others out of love for them. In 2 Corinthians 9:7 we read, "Every man according as he purposeth in his heart, so let him give; not grudgingly, or of necessity: for God loveth a cheerful giver."

We must help our children to understand that the attitudes that motivate their giving are as important as their giving. Jesus taught, "Verily, verily, I say that I would that ye should do alms unto the poor; but take heed that ye do not your alms before men to be seen of them; otherwise ye have no reward of your Father who is in heaven" (3 Nephi 13:1).

As our children come to realize what consecration is, we can help them to look for the needs of others, such as the lonely, shy schoolmate who needs a smile or words of encouragement. As we teach them to have good manners, to turn the other cheek, and to love their fellowmen for what they are—children of God—we also teach the law of consecration.

King Benjamin (Mosiah 4:17-19) cautioned us not to judge or to claim that we don't need to help those in need because they brought their calamities upon themselves. Judging should be left to our Heavenly Father, while we concern ourselves only with aiding others.

Firm Love

As parents we know that it is not wise to give our children everything they ask for. Likewise it would not be wise to give others everything they ask for. And yet we are counseled to give according to others' wants and needs. To answer this dilemma we must understand love.

Love is not a state. Love is a continuum that travels between two poles. On one pole we have gentle love, and on the other we have firm love. In between, on the continuum, there are many degrees or combinations of the two. We can draw this out to make it more graphic for our children.

TYPES OF LOVE

gentle love_____firm love

Too often we talk about, teach, praise, and emulate only the gentle sections of this continuum. That may be because we frequently fear giving firm love. There are many reasons for this, but the most common is that we are afraid of being rejected. When we give love we want to be loved in return.

The Savior taught us both kinds of love and many variations that fall between, but more often than perhaps we realize we see the firm love portrayed in his actions. When he braided a whip and drove the money changers from the temple it was as much an act of love as when he gathered the little children onto his lap and blessed them. It was an act of firm love when God destroyed Sodom and Gomorrah, because the people had refused to repent and had reached the point where that was the only way they could be stopped from increasing the consequences of evil that were engulfing them.

Doing what is best for a person even when it is not what he wants is a display of firm love. Many a person has wallowed in sin because those around him were not capable of giving the firm love he needed in order to climb out of the mucky waters. Gentle love, used at the wrong time, is like quicksand. Instead of giving a path out it sinks the sinner deeper into the mire.

In section 121 of the Doctrine and Covenants the Lord talks about gentle and firm love, how to know when to use each and what to do to assure that our firm love is not misunderstood. Though related here to exercising the priesthood, it seems to be a valid principle for us all.

"No power or influence can or ought to be maintained by virtue of the priesthood, only by persuasion, by long-suffering, by gentleness and meekness, and by love unfeigned; By kindness, and pure knowledge, which shall greatly enlarge the soul without hypocrisy, and without guile—Reproving betimes with sharpness, when moved upon by the Holy Ghost; and then showing forth afterwards an increase of love toward him whom thou hast reproved, lest he esteem thee to be his enemy; That he may know that thy faithfulness is stronger than the cords of death." (D&C 121:41-44.)

Spiritually all people need to learn to stand on their own and not draw upon others indefinitely for the fulfillment of needs. In guiding our children or others to this independence we need all phases of love's continuum. It is neither wise nor loving for us to go about doing everything for everyone. If we did we would deprive others of important growth experiences. So how do we obey the counsel to give in order to satisfy the needs and wants of others? We live in tune with the Spirit and depend upon the promptings of the Spirit to guide our giving.

Sharing Our Precious Gifts

In teaching consecration we should also stress that only by forgetting ourselves and concentrating on others can we really fulfill our own needs. Many people in the world today are trying desperately to fulfill their needs by "drinking" from others, when the only truly effective way to fulfill one's own needs is to fill another's cup. This is a hard concept to illustrate for children. One possible way is to compare life to a bowl of fruit and explain that as a piece of fruit is removed space is created. If we give one apple to sister and one to grandmother and one to a friend, there is a lot of space created in the bowl, and in that space fresh fruit can be placed. If we don't give any fruit away there is no room for fresh fruit, and eventually as we selfishly attempt to keep the fruit it will spoil. Likewise as we give and share with others, blessings come to fill the spaces created by what we give. If we do not share and give there is no room for blessings, and the blessings we already have are taken away or become spoiled.

Another example is to ask a child which is more fun, to give a kiss or to get one, to give a hug or to receive one. When he answers that it is more fun to give a kiss, the parallel can be drawn to the giving of other things.

Under the law of consecration, anything that has been given to us we are in turn obligated to share with others, or we lose the gift. One of the greatest gifts we have, and therefore one of the things we are most obligated under the law to share, is the gospel of Jesus Christ. We must prepare our children to live the law of consecration by teaching them the gospel and how to share it with others.

Jesus was also admonishing us to live the law of consecration when he taught, "Behold, do men light a candle and put it under a bushel? Nay, but on a candlestick, and it giveth light to all that are in the house; Therefore let your light so shine before this people, that they may see your good works and glorify your Father who is in heaven." (3 Nephi 12:15-16.)

As the world in which we live becomes more and more wicked, we as Latter-day Saints have a tendency to withdraw from it. Emotionally, socially, and sometimes even physically we want to build a fort around our families so we can "just live the gospel" and "get to the celestial kingdom." But if we are to fully live the law of consecration we cannot withdraw. That would be putting the bushel basket over the light. Instead we can help our children cope with the influences around them and give to others an example of a better way.

Another thing we should beware of is getting so caught up in the programs of the Church that we fail to be active in the precepts of the gospel. In James 1:27 we are told, "Pure religion and undefiled before God and the Father is this, To visit the fatherless and widows in their affliction, and to keep himself unspotted from the world."

Consecration and Charity

True religion, very simply put, is to live the law of consecration and to keep ourselves free from sin. This takes us back to our original definition of the law of consecration: to set our hearts upon righteousness and to put the kingdom of God first in our lives. This is the higher law, and when we live it we are blessed with charity.

"Charity is the pure love of Christ, and it endureth forever; and whoso is found possessed of it at the last day, it shall be well with him" (Moroni 7:47; see also verse 45).

If we and our children are to be found possessed of this great gift of charity, we need to learn to live the law of consecration. The more fully we live this law, the more charity we will have, and the more charity we possess the easier it is to live the law of consecration. That is why throughout this chapter it has been impossible to talk about one without the other. To illustrate this for my children I draw a circle inside the faith and obedience circle (see chapter 4), and explain that faith and obedience are the first steps to obtaining charity. Then by living the law of consecration we make ourselves worthy to be blessed with charity.

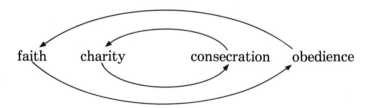

faith   charity   consecration   obedience

Bringing this gift of charity or love into our children's lives is a key to overcoming jealousy, quarreling, and other contentions that often occur in families. As our children give of their time and talents in service to others they will be blessed with this capacity to love. As members of a family serve each other, the home will also be filled with love.

In addition to this, charity is one quality that makes us like our Heavenly Father, and it is by obeying gospel laws and living the law of consecration that we gain charity. As with all gospel gifts, it is also important that we pray for charity. (See Moroni 7:48.)

The higher law of consecration is often the hardest to live, but each of us must live it in order to become a celestial person. By living the law of consecration, we "feed" the seeds of godhood within us, enabling them to grow and mature.

Consecration is also perhaps one of the hardest concepts to teach, but as with all teachings the earlier it is taught the easier it is to live.

Summing Up

In order to understand and live the law of consecration, our children must be taught:

1. that all they are and all they have comes from God.
2. that they are indebted to God for all he has given them.
3. to learn how to work hard and to prepare themselves for service.
4. to identify and then activate and strengthen the gifts within themselves by—
   a. developing and sharing talents,
   b. imparting of material means to the poor and needy,
   c. studying and teaching the gospel,
   d. giving of their time in service to their fellowman and to the Church.
5. to seek after the gift of charity through prayer and by living the law of consecration.

Chapter 8

Step Seven: Enduring to the End

"Behold, I am the law, and the light. Look unto me, and endure to the end, and ye shall live; for unto him that endureth to the end will I give eternal life."—3 Nephi 15:9

Have you ever seen a wood sculptor take a plain chunk of wood and carve it into a masterpiece? It is a painstaking process. As the sharp knife cuts away at the wood, chips fly. Calculated gouges slowly dent the wood. To the unwary spectator, there seems to be no meaning or reason, but after a time the predetermined form begins to appear. It is vague at first, but as the knife continues to cut meticulously away, the wood slowly takes on meaning and character. Finally the object is recognizable, but still there are slivers of wood to be cut away here and a dent or groove to be engraved there. Even then it often takes a hard sanding to give the wood that final finished touch.

Without the cutting and molding and sanding, the object would remain a worthless scrap of wood. But under a master's hands—a master with a specific purpose in every cut, every slit—the wood becomes a valuable masterpiece.

Our lives are much the same as the block of wood—and the great artist sculpting us into masterpieces is God. He doesn't use a chisel or a knife, but the process is just as painstaking and precise, and even more calculated. He is shaping our souls for godhood, and the "tools" he uses to do the shaping are the trials and tribulations we encounter during mortality. The way we handle these challenges determines whether we become masterpieces or mediocre entities: telestial, terrestrial, or celestial beings.

Purpose of Trials

President Joseph Fielding Smith said: "We are in the mortal life to get an experience, a training, that we couldn't get any other way. And in order to become gods, it is necessary for us to know something about pain, about sickness, and about the other things that we partake of in this school of mortality." (*Conference Report,* October 1967, page 122.)

Sometimes even as adults we lose sight of the fact that the primary purpose of this life is for us to be tried and tested. Life wasn't meant to be easy. Mortal life is the time for us to develop faith, spiritual strength, and all the traits of godliness. (See Alma 12:24; D&C 136:31.)

Often we find ourselves avoiding challenges. What is worse, we sometimes protect our children from the challenges that will give them maturity and growth, that will shape them into celestial beings. Problems, challenges, trials, the opposition in life all have a definite purpose (see 2 Nephi 2:11-13), just as the sculptor's knife does. Teaching a child to view these challenges in the proper perspective, to accept them and make the best of them, gives him healthy attitudes that will carry him through life successfully.

We help develop these attitudes as we teach a child to look for the good in situations. We can help him learn that often chastening comes because the Lord loves us and wants us to return to him. Some of our trials come because the Lord knows that these trials will teach us, will strengthen our characters, and ultimately make us better people, even celestial people. The Lord has said, "Whom I love I also chasten that their sins may be forgiven, for with the chastisement I prepare a way for their deliverance in all things out of temptation, and I have loved you" (D&C 95:1). "For all those who will not endure chastening, but deny me, cannot be sanctified" (D&C 101:5).

To help our children endure, we can guide them to recognize the opposition in their lives. Opposition takes on different forms and can vary from physical handicaps to the way other people treat us. Circumstances, people, poverty, failings, and limited abilities are some of the obvious situations that can cause opposition. At other times less obvious things such as wealth, intelligence, popularity, beauty, or talent provide the trials in our lives by keeping us from being humble or from doing the Lord's work. Often opposition and trials are so subtle that we don't recognize them for what they are until it is too late.

It is also helpful to teach our children that enduring doesn't mean doing the right things for a year and then forgetting about them. Enduring also doesn't mean "eat, drink, and be merry, for tomorrow we can repent." Enduring means to start now and to continue in righteousness, overcoming trials one step at a time.

The Importance of Attitude

The story of Joseph in the Old Testament (see Genesis 37-50) is a beautiful example of opposition and enduring. In a few short days Joseph went from favored son of a rich father to Potiphar's slave. But instead of letting circumstances dictate the way he would react, he remained faithful and did his very best. Soon his diligence was recognized and he was made head of Potiphar's household. Then Potiphar's wife tried to seduce Joseph. Humiliated by his rejection, she dishonestly accused Joseph of the sin and he was thrown into prison. Still Joseph endured the persecution. Again in prison he excelled, and was soon made head of the prison. Then circumstances allowed him to interpret Pharaoh's dream and he was made ruler of all Egypt, second only to Pharaoh himself. All this happened because Joseph endured well the trials placed before him.

There are many questions we could ask about this story. After being the favored son of a wealthy father, did Joseph need the discipline of poverty and servitude to prepare him to rule Egypt? Did years spent in prison earn him leadership qualities he needed as a ruler? Did Joseph need to prove to himself what moral fiber he was made of in order to become a great leader? If Joseph had been made a ruler without the ten or more years of trial and tribulation, would he have had the character to withstand the temptations of prosperity and fame?

The trials and tribulations Joseph endured helped make him the great man he was. The story of Joseph is also symbolic of our struggle to live life in order to become celestial beings. We leave our heavenly home, come into a strange world where we must prove ourselves, and then if we prove faithful we will be made kings and queens in God's kingdom.

All of us—no matter what circumstances, what age category—choose, just as Joseph did, how we will react in the situations life places us in. We accept and make the best of our circumstances, even grow and advance because of them, or we complain about our lot in life, resist the opportunities, and never grow.

This is why it is so important that we instill in our children healthy attitudes. Attitudes that are positive, optimistic, and happy will help our children endure to the end.

But there is more to enduring than attitudes. Joseph Smith, while suffering all manner of affliction in the Liberty Jail, was told, "My son, peace be unto thy soul; thine adversity and thine afflictions shall be but a small moment; And then, if thou *endure it well,* God shall exalt thee on high; thou shalt triumph over all thy foes" (D&C 121:7-8; emphasis added).

The Eternal Perspective

Positive attitudes are important, but in order to "endure it well" we need something more, something greater, to cling to. That something is our faith in Jesus Christ. That is the power that sustained Joseph Smith, and it will sustain us. Life's unexpected, often seemingly impossible trials and hardships can only be endured well if we look to that greater hope.

To instill this greater hope, it is helpful to teach our children about eternal perspective. Enduring any trial, no matter how big or how small, is easier when we understand that life existed before mortality and will exist again in a different state after mortality. Today maybe we don't have the material things others have. Today maybe we are in pain. Today maybe we sorrow over loved ones. Today maybe we feel less beautiful, less loved, less talented than those around us. But tomorrow, if we live worthily today, all that the Father has and is has been promised to us.

To help teach this concept of eternity I unwound a ball of white string around our dining room one night. I taped it near the ceiling in each corner so that it circled the room many, many times. Then in one obvious place I made a half-inch black mark on the string. The next morning as my sleepy-eyed daughters entered they were astonished to find the room "strung." They joked about it and asked questions. Then, when I sensed that their curiosity was at a peak, I explained that the string represented the length of our lives and that the black mark represented the small amount of time our mortal existence took up in our lives. We had a good discussion during breakfast and many questions were asked throughout the day that allowed me to review with the girls our purpose for being here, and how death is really only another birth. The most important discussion, however, came as we talked about how the decisions they make each day of this short mortal experience will determine the quality of the eternity that follows.

We can help our children develop this eternal perspective in their decision making by teaching them to ask such questions as: Will this matter in one year; in five years? Will this decision make a difference after this life? Which decision will have the most lasting effects? Will this decision affect my eternal situation?

Even adults often find it difficult to think beyond today or tomorrow, but if we can teach our children while they are still very young to make a habit of thinking beyond this life, many of life's mistakes and hurts can be avoided or at least become much less painful.

Overcoming Daily Discouragements

It is also helpful to recognize and teach that it isn't just the big trials and tribulations that are hard to endure. In times of obvious trial other people often give strength and support to an individual. While the pain or suffering or distress that comes at these times is real, even overwhelming, the outside help and support do help sustain the individual. But in the daily disappointments, the discouragements, the depressing moments that only the person involved knows about, there is often pain and distress but no one to comfort or sustain. Therefore, a big part of learning to endure to the end is learning to cope with these daily discouragements and frustrations.

One of the things that will help us accomplish this is learning not to dwell on the negative. Instead of always thinking about the times we have failed, we must learn to savor and think about the times we have succeeded. If we are succeeding 60 percent of the time and failing 40 percent, we are still succeeding! If we dwell on the 60 percent instead of the 40 percent it can make a big difference in our lives. I've also found it helpful not to think about how far I have to go. That is very depressing! Instead, if we look back at how far we've come since birth, we can be motivated. Slowly—very slowly —but surely there is progression; growth takes place in tiny steps, not giant leaps.

Another thing that I have found helpful in overcoming discouragement is to keep a mental file of good experiences from my past. When I find myself feeling that everything is hopeless and the way is too long, I change the thought and concentrate on one of these stories. One of my favorites to remember is the time my daughter Kirsha went around answering the question, "What is your name?" by saying, "Kirsha, child of God, Johnson." Everyone has moments like these, and if we dwell on them instead of our negative experiences we can endure.

It is also helpful to keep a success list in a journal or some other place. List on it every success you can think of. This is no time to be humble. No one will ever see it but yourself. Make the list as complete as possible, and then every time you experience some success add it to the list. Include such things as, "I gave a very good lesson to the Laurels on March 6," or, "We had an extremely good home evening about honesty. Johnny said..." Nothing is too small or too large for the list. Then, as discouragement creeps up, take out the list and savor it. Enjoy it!

Sometimes discouragement comes as we talk about where we are going, the goal, and how to get there. In lessons, firesides, and other meetings, speakers and teachers talk about the ideal and the place we all want to arrive at. Some people come away feeling discouraged, feeling that they don't measure up. In this circumstance we need to recognize that if we don't discuss the ideal we won't know where we are going. What good does it do to talk about where we already are? If we demand that speakers or teachers come down to a level of "reality" and mediocrity, we deprive ourselves of knowledge that could help us draw closer to the ideal. Achieving the ideal is a process, not an end.

Other times discouragement comes because we are looking for the easy way, gimmicks, or a shortcut to perfection. When someone tells us that the only way to gain exaltation is through prayer, fasting, scripture study, repentance, and obedience to the commandments, we get discouraged because it seems too hard. We want a way that takes little effort, so we label these things as unrealistic and go on searching for shortcuts. However, the principles of the gospel are the only realities. We must learn to use these principles to combat discouragement, not avoid them and thereby cause discouragement.

In dealing with both the major and minor trials in life we should also teach our children that not all of life's obstacles can be overcome. Enduring well in these instances means to make the best of the situation, to smile despite the pain or hurt and go on with a hope and faith in Jesus Christ that all will be better someday. As we take our children through the eight teaching steps and they begin to realize the great spiritual help available to them, they will gain strength from those higher sources to endure whatever trials and tribulations life has for them.

Helps for Enduring

We also make enduring well easier by making a home where the eternal rewards are discussed and looked forward to. We can talk about and stress these great rewards in our daily conversation. King Benjamin said, "And if they hold out faithful to the end they are received into heaven, that thereby they may dwell with God in a state of never-ending happiness" (Mosiah 2:41). And in the Doctrine and Covenants we are told, "And now, behold, whosoever is of my church, and endureth of my church to the end, him will I establish upon my rock, and the gates of hell shall not prevail against them" (D&C 10:69; see also Alma 36:3).

There are also many beautiful scripture stories that can be used to illustrate this principle of endurance. The stories of Abraham, Noah, Job, and Joseph Smith are just a few. The stories of Jonah and Zeezrom are great for showing reluctance, repentance, and finally endurance, and the stories of Balaam, Laman, and Lemuel show what happens to those who do not endure.

One final thing: As we endure and overcome, as we draw close to the Lord, we are sometimes tempted to think that we shouldn't have as many problems or trials. Often we hear a good lesson, go home and try to incorporate the ideas, and then become discouraged because all of life's problems didn't disappear. The toilet still runs over, the children still track mud through the house, the baby is still colicky, the bills are still more than the income, and the patience always wears out before the day does. There is no promise in the scriptures that righteousness ends all problems. The rains fell just the same on the house built upon the rock as they did on the house built upon the sands. Gospel living doesn't mean that the rains will cease. Gospel living only means that the foundation under us will be strong enough to help us endure the storms.

Enduring is also easier when we realize that whenever we make an effort to better ourselves, Satan is going to try to stop us. He doesn't want us to make ourselves better. He will do anything he can to convince us that we can't do it. Because of this it is often during the times we are striving the hardest that we encounter the most problems.

Moroni gave us some good advice and encouragement when he said, "Dispute not because ye see not, for ye receive no witness until after the trial of your faith" (Ether 12:6). If we teach our children to endure—to endure well—they will pass through the trials and receive that witness.

Summing Up

We must help our children endure well by teaching them:
1. the purpose and importance of opposition in their lives.
2. that the Lord chastens those he loves in order to help them grow and learn.
3. to gain an eternal perspective of life.
4. that enduring means accepting what we cannot change and overcoming what we can.
5. that the strength we need in order to endure comes only through trusting in the Lord and living the gospel.

Chapter 9

Step Eight: Doing Things in Order

"To every thing there is a season, and a time to every purpose under the heaven."
—Ecclesiastes 3:1

I once attended a ward in another city, a place with which I was completely unfamiliar. Because of this I had asked for detailed directions to the building and had carefully written down everything I was told. I left fifteen minutes early to assure I would have enough time, and as I traveled I was very careful to follow every instruction I had been given. I exited from the freeway, drove west to the stop light, turned left, and drove two miles. I had been told that the chapel would then be on my left and I "couldn't miss it." But after going two and a half miles without passing a church, I found myself on a dirt road surrounded by mooing, brown-eyed dairy cows.

Carefully I went over my instructions again. I had followed them exactly. Retracing my steps I still found no church. In desperation I stopped at a home to ask new directions and finally found the church.

It wasn't until I was on my way home that I discovered the problem. There were two stop lights after the freeway exit. I had only been told to turn at the light, and so I had turned at the first one when it should have been the second. I was prepared. I did my best. I obeyed the instructions, but I still failed. And because I had turned at the wrong place, it didn't really matter what other directions I followed.

After teaching and speaking to his people, King Benjamin wisely counseled them: "And see that all these things are done in wisdom and order; for it is not requisite that a man should run faster than he has strength. And again, it is expedient that he should be diligent, that thereby he might win the prize; therefore, all things must be done in order." (Mosiah 4:27.)

Some people use this verse as rationale not to work their hardest or up to their potential. But King Benjamin stressed that we should be diligent. We should work and strive as hard as we can—as a matter of fact, we have been counseled to lengthen our stride—but each step must still be taken in the proper order, at the proper pace, and in the proper time. Most of us fail not because we are running too fast, but because we try to take three steps at once or to skip four steps or to take step five before step two. We miss because we try to do things before we have adequately strengthened and prepared ourselves to do them. Therefore it becomes very important that we teach our children to look for, recognize, and then proceed with order, one step at a time.

Years ago we lived in a branch in Germany where the congregation was so small that we were called upon often to speak at sacrament meeting. My favorite subject was the power of positive attitudes in conjunction with achieving goals. After one such talk a man only a few years older than myself approached me with the intention of setting me straight.

"When you're older," he counseled with a condescending smile, "you will understand that what you said is wrong. You haven't lived long enough to realize that you can't just do anything you want in life by thinking you can. There are too many forces playing against us."

I smiled back, "You can if you want it enough and if it is something you have direct control over."

"No," he persisted. "I've lived longer than you and I've wanted a lot of things very much and I've even thought I could do them, but that doesn't make it happen. All that jazz about positive attitudes just doesn't work."

"It does," I said.

"All right, you're saying that if I walked over to the piano and because I believe with all my heart that I can do it then I'll be able to just sit down and play beautiful music."

That was the clue to the problem. Somehow I had not communicated. Positive attitudes are a powerful tool in achieving goals, but they are not shortcuts that will take us to our goals. I had failed to communicate that no matter what our attitude is, we must still climb each stair before the next one will be within reach. Each step is important and must be climbed in the proper order. If a person wants to play the piano, he must start at lesson number one and then practice until he can "just" sit down and play the piano. For some it takes longer than for others, but for everyone order in development is important. A positive attitude is like a hand-rail that helps us up the stairs, but it will not lift us up those stairs.

Step-by-Step Development

This order that King Benjamin counseled us about is an important part of all areas in our lives. The physical order of a child's development is easily seen. First he rolls, then sits, then crawls, and so on. Psychologists have instructed us of a similar pattern in the emotional areas of development. As mothers we often speak of these as stages: tantrum stage, stubborn stage. As with physical development, these stages usually follow a pattern with little variance as to the age during which they occur. As annoying as these stages are, they serve a very important function in the growth and development of the child.

Educators advise us of the same step-by-step process in intellectual development. A child must recognize the alphabet before he can read. He must be able to add and subtract if he is to perform multiplication and division. If a child misses a basic addition concept, multiplication might as well be calculus.

In all areas of growth, step-by-step, ordered development is a must. Each area also tends to overlap into the other areas. Some physical skills are needed before other intellectual skills can be developed. Each step, each stage is vital to future growth. Childhood itself is an important preparation for adulthood. If we rush childhood we endanger adulthood.

A friend of mine learned this concept of order the hard way. She was remodeling an older home when her son was at the crawling stage. Because of the cold, drafty floors she didn't let him crawl, but kept him in a playpen or crib until he walked. When he started school he had trouble reading. Upon taking the boy to a specialist, his parents discovered that his not passing through the crawling stage had left him void of several motor skills needed in order to read. To correct the problem they had to make him crawl around the house several times a day.

As we look to the world around us, we see that all of God's work is characterized by this same order. The life cycle of the living world, the seasons, the process of development in the inanimate world all happen a step at a time, with each step being vital to all that follows.

Likewise our spiritual development and that of our children is built "line upon line, precept upon precept" (D&C 98:12).

As we study the gospel we find that all principles and doctrines fit together like pieces of a jigsaw puzzle. If one or two pieces are out of place or misshapen, the entire puzzle is affected. Nothing else fits with the misshapen piece.

Order in Gospel Teaching

In studying the Old Testament, we become aware of how many questions and problems arise because people's understanding of God is incorrect. They do not know him. They do not understand how he works with and for his children, so they cannot interpret correctly what happened in Old Testament times.

In teaching our children we must have a correct understanding ourselves (step one) and then teach them correct concepts (so the pieces aren't misshapen) one step at a time (so the pieces fit together).

I was once in a meeting in which we were discussing the council in heaven. One man explained that in the premortal council Jesus presented a plan to work out man's salvation and Satan presented a different plan. Several people spoke up saying that Jesus did not present a plan, but volunteered to fulfill God the Father's plan. As the discussion went back and forth the man became upset. It was clear that he thought everyone was nit-picking, which sometimes happens in doctrinal discussions. However, in this case a correct understanding is necessary in order to lay the foundation for other teachings of the gospel.

If we teach our children that Jesus made up the plan, that he thought it up and carried it out himself, then as they are taught to make Jesus their model and to do as he did, they may misunderstand how to use their agency. But if we have taught them that God the Father presented the plan and Jesus offered to fulfill it (see Moses 4:2) and be the Redeemer of mankind, we have a correct foundation for all that follows.

Then when we teach our children to make Jesus their model, to do as he did, we teach them that the only way to return to the presence of God is to obey him. No one, not even the Savior, could make up his own way to salvation. The way is set and we must simply follow.

Most of our frustration in trying to live the gospel comes not because it is too difficult but because we don't understand it well enough. Once we see the overall picture and gain a correct understanding of gospel principles, living the gospel becomes a solution to life's problems, not a problem itself.

It is easy to see that our teachings must be correct if we are to lead our children back to their Father in Heaven. What is sometimes harder is to realize the "line upon line" order of gospel teaching. This is what was so exciting to me about the eight steps of teaching. Each step builds upon the ones that come before it. A person cannot really understand why he should rely upon the Holy Ghost (step five) if he doesn't understand his own divine origins (step two), why we have commandments (step two), how obeying commandments brings faith (step three), and so on. But when a foundation and understanding of those things is firm, a person will have a desire to seek the Spirit which in turn prepares him for steps six, seven, and eight.

When I found the eight teaching steps discussed in this book I was excited because I knew that learning takes place in increments, and these steps broke the gospel into increments. Sometimes we try to feed the gospel to our children a shovelful at a time. But that becomes impossible to digest. The eight steps broke the gospel into spoonfuls that could be taught a bite at a time.

The way I have used these steps is to concentrate on one step each month. I start with step one, preparing to teach, and use the month to evaluate myself, set goals, evaluate the children's needs, and do other things that will help me be a better teacher. As to teaching them during this month, I stress that someday they will be the teachers and that they should be developing the three traits that make a good teacher.

The next months I take the other steps, sometimes trying to cover all the things summarized at the ends of the chapters, and other months zeroing in on one item or part of the step in greater detail. After we cover all eight steps, we start over with step one and go through the cycle again. Sometimes if needed I take a little more than a month, and once in a while even less. In this way, a spoonful at a time, I hope to give my family the whole shovelful.

During each month I use part of my personal study time to review and broaden my knowledge of that month's subject so that the topic is fresh and constantly in my mind. Then I watch for moments to talk about the subject. While running errands, working or playing with the children, I bring up a question or tell a story and discuss it for a few minutes.

In addition to this we have a bulletin board in our dining room that covers the entire wall. I usually put something on the board that correlates with what I am teaching. These displays are usually quite simple: One was just a picture of Jesus with children which I captioned with the question, "What does it mean to be a child of God?" These displays spark conversation and give visual reinforcement to the concepts we talk about.

Sometimes my husband or I will give a home evening lesson about the subject, but for the most part we have found it more effective to let one of the older girls, in partnership with one of the younger ones, choose her own subject and teach home evening.

I have also marked my scriptures by putting the number of a step in the margin beside a verse it applies to. In this way I can quickly find verses of scripture to illustrate with during teaching moments as they occur.

The best part of teaching this way is that it does not take a lot of time. The biggest effort is step one, preparing. After studying and learning ourselves, teaching becomes primarily a matter of looking for opportunities and then taking advantage of them as they come. And it is amazing how many opportunities do come when we concentrate on one principle at a time and then look for ways to teach it as we go about our daily chores.

This idea is summed up in Deuteronomy 11:18-19, "Therefore shall ye lay up these my words in your heart and in your soul, and bind them for a sign upon your hand, that they may be as frontlets between your eyes. And ye shall teach them your children, speaking of them when thou sittest in thine house, and when thou walkest by the way, when thou liest down, and when thou risest up."

Helping Those Who Stray

Another aspect to doing things in order involves dealing with children who have gone astray or husbands whose spiritual development is suffering. In 1 Nephi 2:12 Nephi explained why Laman and Lemuel strayed. He said, "And thus Laman and Lemuel, being the eldest, did murmur against their father. And they did murmur *because they knew not the dealings of that God who had created them.*" (Emphasis added.)

Coming to know our Heavenly Father is step number two. It is a foundation for all other gospel knowledge. Nephi also tells us that his brothers would not pray and ask for confirmation of the things their father taught (also step two). Without this foundation, even a visit by an angel could not convince Laman and Lemuel to love their brother, to be obedient, to consecrate their lives to the Lord.

We can learn much from this story concerning our dealings with and teachings to others who struggle with gospel principles or who are just learning. Sometimes we, like my friend who had to make her son crawl at age six, need to back up and concentrate on the teachings of God's love for the individual. In these cases we need to encourage prayer and help the person come to know that he is a child of God.

Many times we have been admonished by the prophets not to nag or try to force or intimidate those who are struggling or who have forsaken spiritual matters. When we understand order we understand why. As we talked about in step one, love is necessary for a teacher-learner relationship to exist. Nagging, forcing, and intimidation are all negative influences that are contrary to love. When these negative influences are present, the communication of love is hindered, therefore the teacher-learner relationship is jeopardized.

It is also important to realize that change in ourselves or others only takes place after a significant emotional encounter. Love, the most powerful of all emotions, therefore can be our greatest tool in helping change to occur in those around us.

Setting Priorities

Another aspect of doing things in order is to recognize the importance of priorities. We are told in the scriptures of a time when Jesus visited with Martha and Mary. While Martha bustled about the house, her sister, Mary, sat at Jesus' feet listening to all he had to say. Finally, upset at having to do all the work herself, Martha asked Jesus, "Dost thou not care that my sister hath left me to serve alone? bid her therefore that she help me.

"And Jesus answered and said unto her, Martha, Martha, thou art careful and troubled about many things: But one thing is needful: and Mary hath chosen that good part, which shall not be taken away from her." (Luke 10:38-42.)

In our quest for spiritually centered motherhood one of the most important things we can learn and teach is to set and abide by priorities. If we can help our children identify the one needful thing (the gospel) and then make it the priority in their lives, they also will taste of "that good part."

Another part of doing things in order is to recognize that we should not compare ourselves to others. The order or plan for our lives is different than that of our neighbors. We came into life different, we grow differently, we all have a different purpose and mission. In other words, we all have our own order of development. That is a beautiful thing about the gospel: It is tailored to fit each person—exactly! We cannot be doing everything at one time, but if we are in tune, the Spirit will direct us as to what we should be doing at any given time. He may direct one person to do genealogical work, another to serve a neighbor, another to write a poem, another to build a meetinghouse, or another to serve in a civic position. The frustration some feel in trying to live the gospel is that instead of getting in tune with the Spirit and doing at each moment what they are directed to do, they try to do everything at once. They look at everyone around them and try to fit into everyone else's tailor-made mold. Then they feel frustrated when it's too big or too small or rumpled here or there. Some things are standard, such as the prophet's counsel for every young man to go on a mission. But with other things, if we are honest with ourselves, if we are in tune with the Spirit, we can fulfill our mission in life without undue frustration.

One last thing before leaving the subject of order: It is interesting to notice that as we go through steps two through eight ourselves, making our testimonies strong and firm in each area, we accomplish step number one of preparing to teach.

Summing Up

In our efforts to become more spiritually centered, we need to:

1. recognize that there is order in all things.
2. implement a plan that will teach the gospel to our children "line upon line, precept upon precept."

3. back up to steps one and two and begin to teach again, for those who have strayed or not caught the vision.
4. identify priorities and use them to plan our lives.
5. teach that the order or plan for each person is different, and that by seeking the Spirit each person can know of the order his life should take.
6. recognize that by going through steps two through eight we accomplish step one.

Chapter 10

Getting There

> *"All victory and glory is brought to pass unto*
> *you through your diligence, faithfulness, and*
> *prayers of faith."—D&C 103:36*

In our effort to become more spiritually centered, to "get there," we must be sure not only of the route but of the most suitable modes of travel. And we must be careful that we don't admire a particular vehicle so much as to lose sight of the destination. In other words, we must not confuse means with ends. We must not mistake activities for principles.

Principles and Activities

Many years ago at a Relief Society meeting a well-intentioned sister began extolling the virtues of *always* having dinner together as a family. She went on and on and on until her message became overly didactic. "If you don't always have dinner together your children have no chance of becoming righteous," she seemed to be saying. Several people, including me, became squirmish. I was young. My husband had just been called into the bishopric and with him coming and going we didn't *always* have dinner together. I looked around me and saw mothers whose husbands worked shift work, or whose teenagers worked every night after school, but the sister went on.

Finally a sister in the back of the room raised her hand. "I know a mother who has raised ten very special, fine children and who credits her success to the fact that on weekdays they never ate dinner together. Her little ones became hungry around four-thirty or five o'clock, but her husband didn't get home until seven o'clock. Making the little ones wait until seven only made them irritable and ornery. Giving them a snack ruined their appetites. Teenagers were coming and going. Some nights they had to be to Mutual or other places by seven. Her solution was to fix dinner at four-thirty and feed each person when he or she needed to be fed. She visited with each child as he ate, and by the time her husband came home each person's needs were met so the home was peaceful. She and he ate together, then went in and visited with the children."

I stopped worrying and over the years have found that neither plan works for our family. Some nights we eat all together; some nights I plan a staggered meal—but that isn't important. What is important is what I learned from this experience. Sometimes in our eagerness we preach an activity instead of a principle. Eating together had been a wonderful experience for the first sister, and in her joy and enthusiasm she wanted us to have that same experience. But it is communication time together, not dinner, that is important. By looking past the activity (in this case dinner) to the principle (communication time) we often find that we already have the *principle* operating in our homes. If not, we can incorporate it into our lives via an *activity* that is suited to our family needs.

Often a family needs to try several activities in order to find one that works for them. When we first decided to memorize scriptures as a family I underlined in red a particular verse in everyone's book and told them to memorize it. No one could be bothered with opening up the books! Next I typed the verse on three-by-five cards, one for each family member, thinking that after a few years they'd have fantastic scripture files. They lost the cards before a word was committed to memory. Finally I made a big poster of the verse and hung it on the dining-room wall where they see it often, and that has worked for us.

In other cases I've found that what works one time may not work the next time. But by working with principles instead of activities I can merely change the activity to accomplish the same purpose.

To achieve our goal of spiritually centered motherhood we should be filling our homes with principles that have purpose and meaning, not just with activities.

Use the Priesthood

Another important thing that will help us become spiritually centered mothers is to learn to rely upon and incorporate the powers of the priesthood in our homes. As we encourage and ask for priesthood blessings and in all other ways honor the priesthood, we bring great spiritual strength into our homes. We don't need to wait until someone is very ill to ask a husband to give a blessing. We and our children are entitled to priesthood blessings any time we feel a need. When a school year starts, when we are undertaking a difficult task, making an important decision, living under emotional stress, we can ask for priesthood blessings to aid or comfort us.

If the husband is not a priesthood holder, or if the wife and children are alone, then a home teacher or bishop can be called upon. Great power and strength is available to us through the priesthood, if we will only seek it out and use it.

We should also talk with our husbands about the principles discussed here, so that we can "team-teach" our children the gospel. By discussing principles and methods of teaching together, we also come up with new and better ways to approach our children. Two minds are better than one, and so are two teachers.

Stress the Spiritual

Another help in reaching our eternal goal is to emphasize the spiritual side of our lives as often as possible. President McKay said, "Having in our possession the high principles of the gospel as revealed through Christ, why cannot members of the Church at least in the home, in school, in all their associations, emphasize the spiritual side of their natures instead of the carnal side?" (*Conference Report*, April 1958, page 6.)

As we fill our homes and lives with pictures, music, and books that stress the spiritual side of our lives, that show love, goodness, happiness, and beauty, we help accomplish this purpose. Through doing this we also build and reinforce the spiritual qualities within us and our children.

One of my most priceless possessions is a picture a very dear friend painted of me holding one of my newborn daughters. All I need to do when discouraged is look at that picture, and it reminds me of my priorities, of love, of joy! It encourages me. The more we fill our homes and lives with these kinds of things, the easier we make our journey.

It is helpful not only to surround ourselves with encouraging things but to constantly feed the spirit within us. We feed our bodies three times a day (sometimes more!) but often neglect our spirits. Basics like prayer, fasting, the sacrament, and scripture study are food for the spirit, but in addition each of us has personal likes such as taking a walk alone in the mountains, talking to a special person, writing poetry, listening to good music, or reading good books that feed our spirits. It is just as important to give ourselves time for such things as it is to give our children time. As a matter of fact, if we don't take time to fill our own wells we have no water to quench another's thirst. We have nothing to give.

Getting to our goal of spiritually centered motherhood is a long journey. It will not happen overnight, but each step we take also prepares us for eternal motherhood. Because we are daughters of God, and because he is there to help us, *we can* make that journey no matter how difficult it sometimes seems. The most important thing is that we do not give up. By going on, one step at a time, we will make the journey.

And the rewards are many, one of the greatest being mere satisfaction. The Apostle John made a comment about the faithful who had joined the Church. He called them his children, saying, "I have no greater joy than to hear that my children walk in truth" (3 John 1:4). John's comment is applicable to us as mothers also. As we travel the road of spiritually centered motherhood, as we draw closer to our Heavenly Father, we will have "no greater joy than to hear that [our] children walk in truth."

Summing Up

There are several things that will help make our goal of spiritually centered motherhood easier:

1. learn to identify and apply principles, not just activities.
2. draw upon and encourage the power of the priesthood at every possible opportunity.
3. coordinate gospel teaching with our husbands.
4. emphasize the spiritual sides of our lives.
5. feed our spirits regularly and constantly.

Index

Index

— M —

McConkie, Bruce R., on faith, 50
McKay, David O., on spirituality, 19
Man, divine attributes, 95-96
Manipulation, 26
Marriage, interfaith, 4
Married couples, problems, 18-19
Material gifts, 102-3
Maturity, 45
Meditation, 15-16
Misbehavior, consequences, 45-46
Mistakes, acknowledgment, 12
Modesty, 40-41
Mortality, purpose, 111
Mother-daughter relationship, 87-88
Mothers, prayer, 34-35
Musical instrument, practice, 99-100

— N —

Negative thoughts, 115-16

— O —

Obedience, 76-77
Obstacles, 117
Offerings, 103
Opposition, recognition, 112
Order, proper, 121-22, 129

— P —

Parenthood, training for godhood, 31
Parents, responsibility, 3-4
  scriptural instructions, 4
Patriarchal blessings, 16
Perfection, 59
  attainment, 117
Piano practice, 99-100, 122
Plan of salvation, 124
Pondering, 15-16
Popularity, 112
Positive attitudes, 121-22
Poverty, 112
Pratt, Parley P., on gifts of the
  Spirit, 92-93
  on man's divine attributes, 95
Prayer, 31-35
  teaching, 52
Prayers, children's, 17

Preaching, 90
Premortal life, 65
Pretending, 72
Priesthood blessings, 133
Principles, not activities, 131-32
Priorities, setting, 128-29
Privileges, earned, 43-46
Problem-solving skills, 87-89
Problems, acknowledgment, 12
  purpose, 111, 118
Programs, Church, 107
Progression rate, 116
Protectiveness, misplaced, 45-46
Psychology, 82
Punishment, guilt alleviated by, 59

— Q —

Quarreling, 91

— R —

Reasoning, development, 52-55
  recognition, 46-50
Rebekah, 4
Religion, true, 107-8
Reminders, 49
Repentance, agency
  limitations removed by,
  41-42
  guilt-provoked, 58
  teaching, 71-72
Respectfulness, 44
Responsibility, 43, 100
  teaching, 42, 56-57
Resurrection, 70-71
Rewards, earned, 45
Righteousness, enforced, 52

— S —

Sabbath Day, 31
Sacrament, 70
Satan, teaching about, 65-66
Scripture study, 14-15, 35-36, 61-62,
  133
Second Coming, 74-75
Self, sharing, 101-2
Self-discipline, 18-21
Self-esteem, 25-26
Selfishness, 100

139